Short Talks on Huna

Max Freedom Long

Huna Press
126 CAMELLIA DRIVE
CAPE GIRARDEAU, MO 63701 USA

ISBN 0-910764-02-6

P R E F A C E

"I will tell you a secret," says Max Freedom Long in Short Talk No. 8, "if you will take care to spread it far and wide." He then proceeds to give a hint about the effective use of the Huna prayer-action.

"Huna" means secret in the Hawaiian language, and it was Max Freedom Long who uncovered the secrets of the ancient kahunas and made them known to the world through his many books and bulletins.

As groups were formed for the study and practice of the Huna system, Max Long provided study materials in the form of taped lectures. The first series was in the mid-1950's, only one of which has survived. It is an excellent general discourse on "The Need for Understanding and Using Huna" (1957). In the early 1960's another series of Huna lectures was made on tape, numbering twelve in all. It was found that tapes of forty-five minutes or an hour were too long for group listening, but were excellent for individual study. And so, revisions were begun and nine short talks of about twenty minutes each were completed.

It is these short talks that are transcribed for you here.

Max Freedom Long speaks informally to his students about the TEN ELEMENTS OF MAN. As we "listen in" we hear theories and speculations on the origin of man and of the Huna system. But, he always comes back to the TEN ELEMENTS--the three selves with their "shadowy" bodies, three grades of vital force, and the physical body. And always he speaks in practical terms on the use of the Huna concepts.

Huna students of today will find these discussions as helpful now as they were when they were first made nearly a decade ago.

May 20, 1978 --Dr. E. Otha Wingo

For a list of publications and information on membership in Huna Research, Inc., a Missouri not-for-profit corporation, established for the promotion of The Huna Work, send stamped envelope to

HUNA RESEARCH, INC.
Dr. E. Otha Wingo, Director
126 Camellia Drive
Cape Girardeau, MO 63701 USA

SHORT TALK ON HUNA

NUMBER ONE

BY MAX FREEDOM LONG

GREETINGS! This is Max Freedom Long speaking.

THESE SHORT TALKS are intended to tell people about the recently rediscovered HUNA system of Psychology. The system was developed in early Egypt, or may have come from some earlier and all but lost civilization. It contains all that we modern people know of the semi-science of PSYCHOLOGY, and about a third more, that we still have not discovered. It is this additional third that we will discuss at length, for it is of great value.

HUNA--which means "The Secret"--discloses to us the knowledge that man is made up of TEN ELEMENTS OR PARTS. Modern Psychology knows only FOUR OF THESE: the conscious part of mind, the subconscious part of mind, the vital force and, of course, the body in which the man lives and functions.

RELIGIONS which date back to the time when HUNA was already about 4,000 years old were all we had to tell us the nature of man before modern Psychology began to develop about a century ago. Religion gave man only two parts: a body and a soul--a single soul, if you please, although traces of Huna had found their way into various religions, and from the Greek versions of Christianity we have a vague addition to the soul in the form of the "SPIRIT." In India there were vague references to a "lower" and a "higher" SELF as resident in the body of man.

DISCUSSIONS will be in order after this short talk on Huna, and there will be the temptation for some of you to rise and argue that this or that is a fact because such and such a statement is made in "THE WORD OF GOD." Let me say at once and right in the beginning, that RELIGION is no authority to draw upon to prove or disprove things we learn from Huna. Men, and only men, wrote the various religious SCRIPTURES, and the writers of one Scripture did not agree at all with the writers of the several other Scriptures. Religion does not and never did know more than a possible THREE elements of MAN, so we will do well to stop any enthusiastic religionist when the discussions begin if he starts quoting "The Word of God." PLEASE keep this admonition well in mind. Keep the discussions limited to Psychology and the Huna version of it, and you will be able to learn something of this ancient and most valuable addition to your knowledge of yourself and others.

In passing, may I say that Huna contains ALL that is of value in ALL religions. We shall see this clearly as we progress in our examination of the Ten Elements of Man.

* * * * * * * * * * * * * * * * *

Now for the topic for our opening discussion. Let us take up the FIRST OF THE TEN ELEMENTS OF MAN ACCORDING TO HUNA. This is man's BODY. After my talk, you can discuss your ideas of what the body IS, and how it acts as the vehicle of CONSCIOUSNESS.

In a study of Huna you will do well at all times to watch for three things which must be a part of the man--of YOU. These are (1) Something material through which consciousness can ACT. (2) Some form of consciousness to use the material of the body and brain, and (3) some form of FORCE which is used BY consciousness to work with matter. BODY, MIND AND WILL, if you please.

In our first discussion period we will probably all agree that there is a body, although I am well aware that a few religionists will tell us that all is "Maya" or delusion and that nothing has reality. For our purposes shall we say that the body is real--at least as real to us as other things around us.

HUNA TELLS US that man and his body came up through the animal world in some way. This was a stopping of a unit of consciousness in different animal or other life forms on the long ascent from the least conscious life forms to the most--to man himself This was EVOLUTION, and it was believed that man came up as a conscious unit NOT ONLY THROUGH THE WORLD OF CREATURES, but that in him were traces of what we call the "elements" of rain and wind and sun and lightening, of water and stone and air. Man came by easy stages to learn to build the elements into a body to house his sense of SELF, and he used a force or POWER OF WILL to cause the elemental building blocks to fall into place.

The unit of consciousness grew as it

evolved and learned all the many building trades. It learned to make a shell for itself from lime as a sea creature. It learned to work in groups at an early age, and as coral, its groups built great coral reefs of lime taken from sea water. Always growing and learning, the life unit ran the gamut of experience from fish to bird and from mouse to horse.

Finally it had evolved to the point where it could produce a body capable of being used by a HUMAN TYPE OF CONSCIOUSNESS. With this step we have the human body. We are not told by Huna just HOW this last evolutionary step was taken. Instead, we are told to accept the fact that the step was taken, and that a body had finally been developed in which consciousness could have its finest expression.

Man had, at long last, the power to use inductive REASON. At last he was ON HIS OWN. At last he could understand things infinitely better than he could as an animal. At last he could take over the *control of his own life*.

As an animal--all the way up the scale of evolution--a thing which we call "Intuition" ran his life for him and told him what to do and how to do it. As a bird it taught him to build nests at the right time of the year, to migrate at other times, and to do all the bird things.

We do not know what form of consciousness this "Intuition" may be, or whether it comes from something inside the creature's unit of consciousness or from some "elemental spirit" outside the creature but in some way always directing the life forms.

Many stories of the "Creation" of man

were told by the ancients, most especially by the religionists. Every race and people had a version of the creation Story, and some say that the human spirit was first created and then inserted into the newly created body of the man. One story has it that when the human body was made and was ready, an already developed human spirit from Venus was brought and placed in the body.

The early men who were initiated into the secret lore of Huna often had tales to tell that contained parts of the Secret Science. One of these was that when the gods created man, they used two kinds of clay, red and white for the job. In this way he was able to have TWO SPIRITS live in him. We will not go into the Huna terms for these two spirits as yet, but we can say that in modern terms, the man of two colors of clay was made so that he could contain a SUBCONSCIOUS AND A CONSCIOUS pair of minds, or spirits or SELVES. The Huna initiates, called "Keepers of the Secret," believed that these two parts of human consciousness were TWO DIFFERENT AND SEPARATE spirits or souls or SELVES. Later we will see how this belief in two parts of consciousness answers questions left unanswered in modern Psychology.

The SUBCONSCIOUS is an *animal self* living in an animal body, and we, who are the CONSCIOUS-MIND SELF, live as a guest and guide in the body. THE ANIMAL SELF (or low self), has still, like all animals, the INSTINCTIVE GUIDANCE from somewhere to tell it how to grow a body from the moment of conception, and how to digest food and do all the complicated bodily works. However, it seems to be able to handle MEMORY on its own and without too much instinctual help.

It does all our remembering for us, and even carries our memories with it when we die and become disembodied SPIRITS. It lacks the power to reason inductively, and must rely on the conscious self (or middle self) to reason things out.

Also living as a part of our three-spirit family is the HIGH SELF. It has evolved much farther than the lower selves and acts as a GUARDIAN ANGEL over us. It does not live *in the body*, but above and well outside of it. It may travel far away, but it is always in telepathic touch with its man.

There we are with four of the PARTS of man already explained. These are, first, THE BODY; and second, THE THREE SPIRIT SELVES of the man. The Egyptian Keepers of the Secret spoke of these three SELVES as The Father, or middle self, The Son, or low self with its body, and The High Self as "The Holy Spirit." In Christianity we use the Germanic word and say, "Father, Son and Holy GHOST."

When Christianity and other religions borrowed the outer forms of Huna from the earlier Egyptians, they missed one of the great truths and had no "Mother, Daughter and Holy Spirit." But the Egyptians had an inner Huna teaching in which they taught that there are "TWO TRUTHS" of vast importance. This secret lore concerned the fact that everything comes in "twos." Adam was divided promptly into TWO--male and female, but in the later religions the men grabbed all the honors and elevated a male God and a Father and Son without the Mother getting even a mention except as a necessary evil.

There is polarization and sex and endless pairing off in the realm of the TWO TRUTHS. Light and darkness, hot and cold, male and female, the list is long. The Persians borrowed the Two Truths from the Egyptians and missed the rest of the elements. Their religion is one in which the good forces of Light, constantly battle the bad forces of Darkness--making man at war over his own good and evil all the time. The Keepers of the Secret knew that the only sin was that of hurting others or hurting your own body. But the borrowing religionists gradually made up a whole list of "sins." If you did not pay a tenth of your income to the priests and the churches they built, that was a major sin. The lesser sins were listed up to ten or more, as by Moses in his Ten Commandments. The Hindus had a special bit of sin of their own. They taught that "karma" was the law of cause and effect, and that if you "sinned" in one incarnation, you would have to pay for it either at once, or in a following incarnation. If you were sick, it was because you were paying off old karma. AND, it was a sin to try to heal anyone--for so to heal stood in the way of the action of Sacred Karma. The people of India became very much a hopeless people under so stringent a set of religious rules--and have not recovered from it even today. Buddha came along later, and his religion eased the pressure a little. He taught an escape into Nirvana for those who would cease WANTING anything. It was strong medicine and the cure was a very vague one in so far as the goal was concerned. But in his day the people, men and women, gave up everything, became beggars, and took refuge in the sanctuaries which were provided by wealthy converts. Sex was tabooed desire.

Now, AFTER ABOUT 5,000 YEARS, part of us are winning back to the simple and complete system of Huna. We are modernizing the old religions. Many have left the old dogmatic beliefs and have taken up what is misnamed "Metaphysics." "New Thought" is a better name. It and its related cults teach an over-simplification. They say, THINK RIGHT AND YOU WILL BE RIGHT. This is fine so far as it goes, but it lacks all the things that the ancient Huna System can tell us of WHO thinks, and HOW, and WHY. It has little to say about even one SELF or Soul. God is hardly ever mentioned in the services. In one denomination everything is said to be unreal except the ALL GOOD, and therefore anything that is bad is NOT real. Declare the unreality of bad things and they will cease to be.

These modern departures from old religions and dogmas are excellent in so far as they go. But there are some of us who want to know the HOW's and the WHY's. Who is to do the thinking, the subconscious or the conscious, or are we to drop these for the older idea of JUST ONE SOUL, and let it do all the "right thinking" that brings--mysteriously--"right conditions"?

Let us try to get into a nutshell the secret of making this modern way of doing WORK. First, we must stop making our low selves THINK we are sick. If we hold the picture of ourselves as ILL, we scare the low self all the time and we impress on it the picture of illness--and it has a way of *making the body match the fears*. In France in the last generation, Dr. Coué taught people to THINK of themselves as HEALED. He administered fine "suggestion" to them in which he talked to their low selves over the heads of their middle selves, assuring the lesser spirit that he and his body would be getting well. He had his patients repeat frequently, day after day, the words that *embody the health picture*. Those words are just as good today. They are, "Every day, in every way, I am getting better and better." At one time this formula was all the rage the world around. But it failed in its promise and people soon stopped using it. What was wrong? The answer is simple. The middle self was reciting the words, and the low self was listening. But the middle self did not make the proper mental picture of the man as being healed better and better every day in every way. The middle self didn't make the picture of the *healed condition and live up to it--live IN it steadily*.Here is the key to the failures. FAITH. BELIEF. If you, the middle self, are not fully convinced that you will get better each day and that you ARE GETTING BETTER each day, then neither will the low self believe it. And if the low self does not believe it, it will not stop trying to make the body match your picture of sickness and will NOT START MAKING THE BODY MATCH THE NEW PICTURE OF THE HEALED STATE.

Yes, the low self will heal all kinds of things if let alone. When we break a leg, we EXPECT it to knit the bone for us. So, all goes well and the break is healed. But if we keep frightening the low self with our thoughts of possible ills, it will soon be making bodily changes to match the mental picture.

Next. The High Self helps the low self to change the body to fit the healed picture if we ASK IT TO DO SO. It can work miracles, and often does, for us. It can *materialize* pictures of health and success and peace for us if we will make the mental pictures to fit and have FAITH that they will be *materialized* in due time. "HOLD THE FAITH" is the second part of the key. Realize that you are a Triune or three-spirit being. Work mightily to get all three of your SELVES materializing the SAME good things. Aloha. MFL

* * * * * * * *

QUESTIONS AND ANSWERS

Q. IS the subconscious as large when it starts evolving as a one-cell creature as it is in man?
A. It would not seem likely. Huna tells us nothing on that point. But in the body we see billions of cells of different kinds united as in a great colony and working together for the good of the whole. Perhaps others would like to give their speculative guesses as to the growth of the low self and decide whether it is made up of all the units of consciousness of all the billions of bodily cells.

Q. When we ask the High Self to help us and the low self to materialize the conditions we desire, do we just pray to the High Self? Why can't we just pray to God instead? Doesn't all prayer go to God anyway?
A. In Huna we learn that there are layers and layers of rising consciousness, so to speak. The High Self is in a level higher than the middle self. But above it are still other levels, and Supreme God is so high and so vast that the human mind cannot grasp its Being and Verity. The Keepers of the Secret taught that our prayers always went first to the High Self, and that if they needed to go to a still higher Being, they would be sent on up. But as all of our prayers go to the High Self, the efforts are not wasted no matter to what Higher Being we address our prayers. The prayer to the High Self is made by holding before it the picture of the thing we want it to materialize. In later talks this will be discussed in detail. Would

others care to say what they think about the Huna-type prayer, or about prayer in general?

Q. If we are "Sparks of the Divine," why do we have to try to get the low and High Selves to help us? Why can't we materialize things for ourselves?
A. For several centuries we have been taught in some circles the dogma that "Ye are gods." We have been trying all that time to make things come true to fit our plans and desires all by ourselves--perhaps with a prayer now and then for good measure. The middle self has great ability and can often accomplish great things, but, if we are to accept the Huna beliefs, we will then try to get ALL THREE OF OUR SELVES to cooperate and work on plans and problems. If one is content with the results obtained in the first way, then there is no need to try the second. But most of us often feel that we could do with a little extra help. Does anyone have a comment on the matters?

Q. Where do the low and middle selves live in the body, and are there some special parts of the brain that each uses?
A. There is much speculation as to this. No special organs or parts of the brain have been decided upon as centers of the subconscious and conscious. The ancients were not very definite as to this point in human physiology. They spoke of the low self as residing in the body and the middle self as living in the head. The low self was said to have the memories as its pet possession. The middle self was the proud owner of speech. No animal can talk. It was said that only when the middle self was able to act as a guest in the bodily house, did the human animal talk. The Egyptians made a god of the power of speech. It was "The Word," and in Christianity we meet the idea in a very similar form. "In the beginning was the Word." Any ideas on this?

BIBLIOGRAPHY

The Works of Max Freedom Long:

Recovering the Ancient Magic (1936, 1978)

Introduction to Huna (1948, 1975)

The Secret Science Behind Miracles (1948, 1954)

The Secret Science at Work (1953)

Growing into Light (1955)

Self-Suggestion (1958)

Psychometric Analysis (1959)

The Huna Code in Religions (1965)

Mana, or Vital Force (1949, 1976)

Short Talks on Huna (1978)

Tarot Card Symbology (1960, 1972)

HRA Bulletins (1948-1958)

Huna Vistas (1959-1970)

Other Books Related to Huna:

Andrews, Lorrin, *A Dictionary of the Hawaiian Language* (1865, 1974)

Hickey, Isabel M., *It is ALL Right!* (1976)

Hoffman, Enid, *Huna: a Beginner's Guide* (1976)

Westlake, Aubrey T., *The Pattern of Health* (1961)

Wingo, E. Otha, *Letters on Huna: a Course in the Fundamentals of Huna Psychology* (1973)

SHORT TALK ON HUNA

NUMBER TWO

BY MAX FREEDOM LONG

GREETINGS! Again this is Max Freedom Long speaking.

IN THIS SERIES OF SHORT TALKS we are considering the ancient HUNA or "Secret" System which has been traced back to early Egypt, and which spread from there around much of the world, always being in the hands of initiated priests, but with the inner or really secret teachings eventually lost. It was best preserved in the islands of Polynesia, and was recovered there, at least in large part, during the past century.

In the first talk I told you that we would study the TEN ELEMENTS which Huna tells us make up the MAN (And the WOMAN, TOO--and don't you forget it.)

To review: THE FIRST ELEMENT IN MAN is the body; then we count THREE separate and independent SELVES OR SPIRITS, who make use of the body during life. We also count three ghost bodies which are invisible but made of very fine material and are practically indestructible. These surround the three SELVES during life--surround also the body, except for the one belonging to the High Self, whose "shadowy body" is just attached to the dense body by means of a "silver cord"--a cord made of the same substance as its "shadowy body" (AKA it is called in Huna). When we die we leave the dead body and continue to live in the shadowy bodies, invisible to the eye, but still very real. Lastly, we count three grades of vital force, called in Huna, MANA. Each of the three spirits takes its share of the mana from the physical body where it is created from the food we eat and the air we breathe. Each SELF uses its mana in a different way and for a different purpose. We will come to that in a later talk, but in passing, let me say that the High Self can use its mana to make changes in physical matter, as in the control of heat in fire-walking. It works the miracles for us, In the great mystery play of initiation which was later mistakenly supposed to be real history, the leading character explains, "Not I, but the Father. He doeth the works."

This is pretty dry. Take a few deep breaths and get awake again so I can tell you more about the shadowy body. It is made of such fine material that it cannot be seen, but every time we think a thought, we take some of this substance which surrounds the body and interpenetrates it, and make it into a microscopic THOUGHT-FORM. The low self does this automatically. It ties these thought-forms together in strings and stores them in the shadowy body AS MEMORIES. If something frightens or impresses you greatly, it will cause very large and enduring thought-forms to be made, and these we can easily remember for years. But the average little string of invisible forms, such as one makes in reading bits from the morning paper are stored away and the low self soon forgets where it put them.

AN EXPERIMENT can be performed at your leisure to prove that a big thought-form string is more easily remembered than a small one. The thought-forms are made by the use of the mana by the low or subconscious self and mana is made by breathing more deeply and slowly--that is, you can make a larger charge of it and can then get the low self to use it. Select a few lines of verse to memorize. Time yourself and take five minutes just as you are to memorize the selected lines, say the first verse of a poem. Then take some slow, deep breaths--take four at a time, pause a few seconds, and repeat until you get charged up--usually this can be done in about four of the four-breath series. When charged, take five minutes to memorize the second verse of the poem. Good. Next day see which verse you recall best.

A young friend of mine who learned slowly was taught to breathe the Huna way to help him in his studies. It worked and soon he was "inhaling" all his lessons. One day he was trying to teach his dog to sit up and shake hands, but without visible results. "Oh, rats!" he exclaimed, when I questioned him. "Spotty will never learn. I can't get him to inhale his lessons. He just pants all the time, and never learns a thing!" My former friend, Dr. Rice, who had wonderful success reforming wayward boys and girls, once told me that he had never failed once if he could get his charges to breathe more deeply and correctly. If YOU want to understand what I am trying to tell you with this tape, don't sit there holding your breath, falling to sleep, and not remembering a thing I say. BREATHE IN EVERY WORD, and you'll have something useful to remember--and USE.

Remember the Huna adage: "NO MANA--NO LASTING MEMORY."

The reason a hypnotist's words of suggestion work is that he puts mana into the thought-forms of the words as he plants them in the mind of the relaxed and slow-breathing subject. It isn't the "will" of the hypnotist; it is the MANA. Sleep-suggestion by means of phonograph records gets poor results because there is no mana in the words which are mechanically spoken. In Yoga the valuable part is the full breathing and accumulating of prana or mana, but most Yoga students don't know what do do with the extra mana when they have accumulated it. Yoga started with Huna centuries ago, and then forgot what it was all about. Originally, Yoga taught one how to get into touch with one's own High Self whenever desired, to give it a gift of extra mana, and then get it to give some miraculous help. Or, one just gave the gift of mana as an offering of deep love and devotion. The High Self is "The god within" and deserves all the love and devotion you can give it. It is your heavenly Father and Mother combined. You are the beloved Son "in whom I am well please," if you have been behaving yourself.

The subconscious or low or animal or body SELF is also to be loved deeply and cared for. To IT, YOU--the middle self--are its Father and Mother. It looks to you for love and understanding and guidance--for help when it gets into trouble. It serves you ever so willingly and faithfully, and will use its instinctive abilities and talents in most amazing ways in answer to your requests--if you only will get acquainted with it and learn how to work with it. It is like a bashful and silent child hiding in most of us, and when we begin to try to get acquainted with it, it has a tendency to get behind you and hide like a child hiding in its mother's skirts. These days, if you are a girl and wear a mini-skirt, of course, your low self may not be able to hide from you so well.

The best way I know to get acquainted with your low self is to teach it to use a pendulum and hold little yes-no-doubtful conversations with you through the ways in which it can swing the pendulum. "Yes" is a vertical swing of the pendulum. "No" is a horizontal swing. "Doubtful" or "I do not know" is a diagonal swing. "Good" is a clockwise-circle swing. "Bad" is a counter-clockwise-circle swing. Remember that the low self can help you to speak words, but of itself, it cannot speak. The pendulum allows it to talk to you with the only words it can--symbols. Tie your ring to a five inch thread and it will be a pendulum ready for use. But don't expect results when you start asking the low self to talk with you. Give it time to get over its bashfulness and learn the new trick. But usually it will learn in a few patient sittings and after that will talk happily. BUT, don't ask it to predict future events and then believe what it says, for it cannot see the future and will only make wild guesses in answering. Usually, it will give you the answer that it thinks you would like. Only the High Self can see into the future, and to get that information from it is indeed a fine art.

Later on you may want to work with your low self to dowse for water, or oil, or to map dowse for lost things or persons. It can also make fine Psychometric Analysis readings for you, once you have taught it the code it is to use via the pendulum and the simple Biometer. Don't underestimate the ability of the Younger Self and at the same time do not ask it to do something that only the High Self can do.

Let us get back to the subject of the three shadowy or AKA bodies, for an understanding of them is very necessary to round out our knowledge of just what uses we can make of the ten elements in ourselves and in all human beings. The shadowy body is an amazing thing, especially the one belonging to the low self. We moderns have borrowed from Theosophy the "double" and the "astral body." We indulge in loose talk about "auras," seldom having a very definite idea of what is meant.

It must have been very difficult for the ancient sages to find a good code word or symbol to use to stand for the shadowy body of the low self--to stand for a thing which had so many functions and uses. In the end they selected the code symbol of an umbrella for the shadowy bodies of the three spirits, and when we read about the shadowy body in the hieroglyphics or picture writing of early Egypt, we find that the picture of a raised or fully opened umbrella stands for the aka or shadowy body. Why was the umbrella such a good code symbol? Because the umbrella casts a shadow, and that is something that can be seen and still is invisible in its own way. A shadow is "something." So is the shadowy body--a something real but not to be seen or caught in the hand. For the three shadowy bodies of the three selves, the Egyptians wrote three umbrella glyphs in a row. Their name for the shadowy body was just "shadow." It was the "ka" in Egyptian, or the "a-ka," as the glyph left the vowels out of the written word and these had to be supplied by the reader. In Polynesia, where the art of writing was lost, the full word was preserved, and it is "aka."

The umbrella has a handle to support it, and this handle is a very important part of the code symbol, for it indicates the cord of shadowy-body substance that runs from the aka of the low self to the aka of the High Self. Turn your umbrella upside down and you have then the symbol of the "silver cord" running upward from the low to the High.

All this would sound rather foolish to us, were it not that this "silver cord" of aka substance is our means of contact with our High Selves. It is the telephone line we use when we call up to ask for help or just to say, "I love you." The telephone wire or cord has mana for its electricity, and mana flows from the low to the High Self and back again when we use the mystic phone in prayer or worship.

The same substance, aka, is given the code name of "sticky" (or <u>pili</u>) by the Polynesian inheritors and preservers of Huna. And that describes an almost amusing characteristic of the substance. When you shake hands with someone, your aka body sticks to theirs, as if you had stuck your wads of gum together and pulled them apart, pulling out long threads of gum. These threads of aka substance will stretch and stretch, and under certain circumstances, a number of them will serve as a phone line between two people and enable them to communicate telepathically. Telepathy is the conversation of the two people along the telephone wire of aka substance. It is the same mechanism as is conversation with the High Self. And this leads us to something to be well "inhaled" and made into a good memory. It is that ALL PRAYER IS TELEPATHIC, and ALL TELEPATHY IS MADE UP OF MESSAGES SENT IN PICTURE FORM BY THE LOW SELF!

If your wife sends you a telepathic message to bring home a pound of butter, the low self transmits the message in picture symbols, NOT in words, for it cannot use WORDS. It gives you a picture of your wife and follows that with a picture of her wanting butter. You don't know HOW you get the impression, but you know you got it. You bring home the butter.

All of our prayers are given first to the low self. It changes our wants into pictures, and sends the pictures telepathically, along the aka cord, to the High Self.

If you picture yourself as in perfect health and impress that on the low self as the thing to send as a "want" to your High Self, it will make a picture of you in perfect health, and will send the PICTURE. The way the High Self answers the prayer is to "make real" or "materialize" the PICTURE for you. This is the secret of secrets in Huna. It is what it is ALL ABOUT.

But get this. The picture of perfect health must NOT be one that includes your sickness. If you pray, "Heal my illness," the low self will make a picture of you sick and miserable and send it for the prayer. With it will go a picture of you wanting something, perhaps still another picture of you NOT being sick. The result is a muddle and nothing is given to the High Self to use to change your condition.

In the great drama of Huna initiation,

Jesus instructed: "Ask in faith, believing, ..." etc. Modern New Thought got the idea and teaches us to use the positive affirmation, "I am perfectly well and strong and comfortable." Dr. Coué taught the positive picture in his invaluable formula," Every day, in every way, I am getting better and better." He pictured the getting well process. But better still would be, "Every day in every way, I have perfect health." And, we must have faith. We must believe that we are getting perfect health. We must hold the thought of ourselves perfectly well. If we don't, we send a sick picture inevitably to the High Self to spoil the good picture of perfect health we have already sent up in prayer. It is like pulling yourself up by your boot straps, but it is also the difference between the prayer which gets answered and the one that does not.

Making the picture of perfect health must be done with the use of the mana to get a lasting memory or thought-form picture to keep recalling and sending frequently to the High Self as your prayer. Make and memorize your picture with breathing to collect the mana to give the picture strength enough to hold together while the High Self MATERIALIZES it into actuality for you. Make your picture as if "inhaling a lesson," and don't be like the dog, Spotty, who just sits there and pants.

Tell your low self to send the picture and plenty of mana to the High Self--like a telepathic message. It knows how, so just set it to work. Repeat your prayer-action at least once a day, and keep at it until the answer is given. Have faith. Tell yourself perfect health is already given on the level of the High Self and is already real. Live in the picture. FEEL it. Keep your mind off your ills as off the Devil. You have now the key to real magic. It is yours to use if you will.

Aloha, MFL.

* * * * * * * * * * *

QUESTIONS AND ANSWERS

Q. Was the idea of the silver cord and threads known also in early India?
A. Yes. In Yoga there was the practice of trying to generate a mana or prana force in the sacral region and make it move upward through the centers along the spine, then on up through the top of the head to the High Self. The secret knowledge got all distorted in time, but we still find in the earliest Yoga writings the mention of the "thread soul," which was the low self. The Brahmins still wear the "sacred thread" around their necks, while this same thread idea appears in various other religions in the string of beads worn around the neck. Good Catholics wear a small chain around their necks with a small cross attached, and are very reluctant to remove it night or day. In ancient times there was much borrowing back and forth between religions.

Q. Did the early Egyptians know about the cord or threads?
A. Yes. In some of the drawings in the tombs we see a spider pictured hanging by a thread of web above the mummy case. The spider was the symbol of the aka or shadowy thread at its best. In the outer teachings it was said that one had to climb a thread of spider web in order to get up to heaven. The cord that goes between the body and the High Self is made up of many threads, these

forming a cord--the "silver cord" mentioned once in the Old Testament of the Bible. In Huna the web with the spider in the center, and with web threads reaching out in all directions, was the favorite symbol used to describe the mechanism. In Tibet there was once a whole system of belief developed in which the universe was said to be like a web,and the souls of men like tiny spiders dotted here and there over the vast web. The Aborigines in Australia still have a sacred "string" which is part of their magic kit. In Easter Island the umbilical cord was the symbol, and such cords were carefully preserved after birth. In Polynesia the word for low self had several meanings, one of which was "sticky." This refers to the aka threads, which, like the thread of web exuded by a spider is at first sticky and will adhere to anything--thus making it possible to hang a web between twigs or in the fine space behind a picture.

Q. Why should we send mana to the High Self when we ask for something?
A. The High Self draws from the body, through the silver cord, the mana it ordinarily needs to live in its shadowy body. But, when we ask it to make changes in our so-dense, earthy world, or the conditions in it, the secret teaching is that much more mana is needed--just as when we breathe more strongly to get ready to "inhale a lesson." We accumulate the needed mana and send it to the High Self to use. Of the three selves, only the low self has a physical body capable of creating the life force or mana from the food and water and air we consume. The prayer of the Great Drama, "Give us this day our daily bread," should read, "Let us give YOU each day YOUR daily bread--or mana." The Chinese knew

that the spirits of the dead have but little mana, and so the ancestral spirits were fed--outwardly with food placed on the graves. The inward or secret meaning of this was lost. In Egypt the food of the gods or High Selves was symbolized by honey, and honey was secreted by the bee, so they had a sacred bee in the pictures painted in the tombs. Mana, when accepted by the High Self, was honey. The symbol of the High Self was LIGHT. Its symbol was the SUN.

SHORT TALK ON HUNA

NUMBER THREE

BY MAX FREEDOM LONG

Again, this is Max Freedom Long speaking.

This is the third talk on the ancient SECRET or HUNA system which is first found in Egypt in the early dynasties when glyphs were used for writing. The Secret Lore spread more or less over the then civilized world, and after some 5,000 years as a priestly secret, known only to initiates, it was threatened by loss or complete extinction as a system.

Reginald Stewart, my close friend of the 1936 days when we were struggling to find out what the "SECRET" contained, ran into a tribe of Berber shepherd people in North Africa who could tell him much about the ancient lore. The Queen of the little tribe was an initiate "kahuna" or "Keeper of the Secret," and it was from her that Mr. Stewart gained much secret information which he later passed on to me to assist in my effort to recover the amazing system of Psychology-plus-Religion.

The Berber "Queen Quahine" or "woman kahuna" said that her people had, many centuries earlier, lived in Egypt and had known the SECRET and been able to use it in many wonderful ways. She claimed that it was her people who stood by when the Great Pyramid was being built, and used their magic to levitate the great stones into place.

Important to us is the legend she recited in which at about the year 100 B.C. the Keepers of the Secret looked into the future and foresaw the fact that their beloved lore was on the verge of becoming lost. Much alarmed, they used their fine psychic powers to look about the world for a place to which the Huna tribes could move--and in which they would find safety for the Sacred Huna Lore--find a place out of the world where Huna could be preserved and passed down from parent to child without danger of loss or great contamination.

The legend goes on to say that through psychic vision, the kahunas saw the empty islands of the Pacific, and that they would be the best sanctuary. So, the word went out that all eleven of the little tribes of HUNA people were to leave Egypt and go in big double canoes down the Red Sea into the Indian Ocean, and then make their way as best they could to the far Pacific Isles.

There were, she said, TWELVE TRIBES, but her tribe remained behind as a rear guard lest the others be detained by the rulers of the period. For, be it well understood that people who could work magic were valued and would not be easily allowed to depart, carrying their secret knowledge with them.

When the eleven tribes were on their way, the twelfth tried to follow, but it was too late. They were headed off and forced to go north overland to find safety. They eventually reached what is now Berber Territory and there found a region so safe that, with the help of their magic, they were able to keep alive and also to preserve the Secret

Lore for as long as did the other tribes who had fled to what we now know as Polynesia. These tribes, she declared, were the original LOST TRIBES OF ISRAEL--which have never been found.

The eleven tribes which got away divided, some going along the coast to stop in India for a time and there teach the local priests the SECRET before moving on to the far destination. At least one tribe went along the coast of Africa and came to Madagascar. There at least part of them settled, and even today, half the people of that large island are of the same blood as the Polynesians and speak the same general language. From this place, or spreading from Egypt, a certain amount of the SECRET moved slowly into Africa. There it mixed with local beliefs and superstitions, but can be identified in the lore of witch doctors.

The Berber tribe found by Mr. Stewart had come to speak the Berber way, but the Queen still knew the old Huna words and had to use them in sharing her lore with Stewart, for, as she said, there were no words in other languages to fit the Ten Elements of Huna. Young Stewart, who was adopted as a blood son before being taught Huna, took down in his note books the words of the Huna language used by the Queen in teaching him, and years later, when he began to help me unravel the Secret, he passed on words from his yellowed note-book pages--words which were almost identical to the dialect now used in the Society Islands in the South Pacific.

He was started on his slow way to become an initiate kahuna, as was the daughter of the Queen, and one of the things which they were promised was that in due time they would be introduced to the great nature spirits who watch over and control the lesser creatures and the elements. They would be "ordained" in a ritual way, and after that could make contact with the spirits for themselves and request favors.

The Polynesian kahunas knew the same spirits--totem spirits or gods, if you will--but in the mountains of North Africa, the Queen could not call to the spirits of the sharks and turtles and ask them to do her bidding. Instead, she called to the spirits overlooking the local birds, and requested that all the birds within a certain distance be made to gather where they sat on a high hill and waited.

Soon birds of all kinds began to arrive and light on the ground around them. Big birds and little, they all came. Stewart said, in telling the story, that he was amazed at the number of assorted birds living in that small territory. The birds, once through coming in, were greeted by the Queen, thanked for coming, and given permission to depart--which they did in orderly and unhurried fashion.

On another day the snakes were called in, and a surprising number came wiggling into their charmed circle, to be admired, spoken with, and in time thanked and sent on their way.

Unfortunately, Stewart was never ordained or "introduced" to the totem spirits. Nor was he able to learn more than a beginning of the lore of the Ten Elements, for the Queen was accidentally killed by a stray bullet one day when two feuding groups of Berbers fought through the valley below the place where the Queen's little tribe was encamped. No other teacher was available, and Stewart was forced to give up hope of being initiated, and return home to England. It was many years later when Stewart came across my first book on the lost lore of the kahunas, and in it recognized the nearly identical words which he had been taught and which he had written down in his notes. It was through his aid that I was able to learn the nature of the third spirit of man--the High Self or Superconscious. Also, some help was given in understanding the nature of the vital force, mana. Among other demonstrations made by the Queen before her untimely death was the accumulation of a large surcharge of low mana and the use of it to push a heavy door through the frame and into a temporary storage cave.

Mana is not quite like static electricity or the kind we generate with our chemical batteries. Nor is it like the electricity generated by our power plants. Other forms of electricity want to go places and produce a current. Static electricity is the nearest to mana in its nature. It will charge an accumulator and the charge will remain there for a time. But it will leap at the chance to discharge. The low mana or that manufactured by the low self in the body is like a static charge in that it charges the body and stays put until used.

In my Second Talk I spoke of how mana was to be accumulated by breathing more deeply for a time. I might add that when the breathing is being done, the low self must be expected to build up a mana surcharge in the body and in the shadowy body or aka which surrounds it. I told of the use of the "extra" mana in making strong thought-forms and thus in making lasting memories. In passing, may I say that sight is made temporarily better by putting on an extra charge of mana. If one is tired, a pause to charge up helps greatly, and surprising help in remembering has been reported from students who put on an extra charge now and then while taking an examination.

There is still much testing and experimental work to be done before we will know as much about the manas--the three manas--as did the old initiates. For instance, in Hawaii in the old days the kahunas helped their friends in inter-sectional fighting. They stood behind the fighting lines and charged up sticks with low mana. These they threw over the heads of the men of their side, and when a stick touched one of the enemy, the mana discharged like a great charge of static and knocked the man cold. Women trained for the task also stood behind the battle lines and when a warrior was too spent to carry on, he fell out of the rank and one of the women recharged him quickly with mana so he could get back into the fray with club and spear.

Mesmerism is a similar use of the mana surcharge. A few years ago a Mesmerist in Los Angeles used to demonstrate his power by charging up, then pointing his finger at one after another of the volunteer subjects seated in a row. Each one, when pointed at, would slump and slide from his chair, to remain on the floor for a minute or two and then revive. The heavy surcharge of low mana, when commanded by the operator to go all at once into a subject, acts as if alive and does so, causing the low self to lose consciousness for a short time. In contrast, hypnosis is the use of the mana of the middle self and is used to implant thought-form clusters as "suggestions," with sleep or the unconscious and rigid state caused by suggestion and not by mana shock as in mesmerism of the drastic kind just described.

The low mana, when filling shadowy substance and when *directed by the consciousness*, becomes, to all intents and purposes, *intelligent force*. It can solidify the aka substance, and the spirits of the dead often come to seances and use mana which they borrow from the sitters. With it they can make trumpets sail through the room and tap people on head or knee while causing voices to sound through the trumpets. They can lift living persons and carry them about. This is called "levitation." Many mediums have been levitated in remarkable ways, and some carried to places at a distance. Poltergeists seem to be spirits bent on mischief who get hold of mana and use it to throw things, to make crashing noises, lift heavy furniture, even start fires and throw water.

The use of a mana charge in a single great effort makes it possible for spirits to lift things as heavy as a grand piano, or even to shake the house. A little mana goes a long way when all of it is spent at once in causing something to move. In seances the spirits sometimes produce what we call "apports" by taking a thing--even a person--at a distance, changing it into an invisible state or form, and bringing it into the seance room, there changing it back into its solid or natural form. The High Self of the spirit may well be helping it in the work, for it has the power to make such changes in matter. My friend, Mr. Stewart, speculated that perhaps the lifting of the massive stones for the easy building of the Great Pyramid may have been done by kahunas with the aid of spirit friends who were given much mana and set to work.

If you want a simple use of mana--if you do not wish to study to be a mesmerist, hypnotist, spirit medium, or perhaps a builder of pyramids--the one I can recommend most highly is its use in healing. You may be a natural healer and not know it. Or you may be able with a little practice to develop fair healing powers. If you wish to make a test of your abilities, you must be willing to practice a little to teach your low self what it is to do. With practice it will learn, and after a few successful healings, confidence will be gained--FAITH, in your own power gained--a faith that can make all the difference.

There are three main steps to be taken, once you find a friend with an aching head or a pain of not too chronic a nature. Try simple ills at first, and don't be like one of my friends who learned the art and boasted that he could heal or at least better anything except a "pain in the neck" (of the kind produced by boredom). Cuts, burns and breaks are good to practice on, and with daily treatments with mana, a surprising response may be brought about. The kahunas of old could often heal a broken bone in a few minutes. Mana hastens the healing process greatly if properly applied.

The first step is to do the breathing which I have described earlier, and as you breathe deeply and slowly and rhythmically, silently asking your low self to manufacture a large mana charge. Keep in mind the fact that you plan to use the mana for healing your friend. Also keep in mind the fact that you are going to ask your low self to call upon your High Self to help during the healing.

When you feel that you are well charged up, make a *mental picture* of yourself and your low self causing the patient to be in PERFECT HEALTH; then picture the call being made to your High Self. Don't talk the picture as that just makes words, and the low and High Selves need PICTURES constructed of mana-strengthened thought-forms. Keep your mouth shut and your mind open. The picture is your plan, your blueprint, your road map. BUT, it is also the MOLD which will be used to remold the conditions into health.

With the picture in mind, advance to your patient and place your fingers lightly on the place which hurts or which is injured and needs healing. If the place is not to be touched for one reason or another, first touch the hand or head of the person, then hold your hands at a small distance from the body and on either side of the seat of the trouble. The low self can project the mana through the shadowy thread the touch establishes if you mentally request it to do so. While holding the hands in position, hold your picture in mind of the call going to your High Self, then of the mana flowing through your fingers and into your patient to charge up the part to be restored.

The treatment can last a minute or two, and then you can pull away, recharge with mana, and repeat the treatment--several times if you like and if it takes that many times for the patient to report a feeling of being helped. End by giving thanks silently to the High Self and then to the low, after which go wash your hands and tell yourself that you are washing all the illness or imperfections down the drain, never to return. This will keep you from possibly picking up the pains through suggestion. Remember that you are PRAYING for the healing and also furnishing the mana which the High Self may use. This is one of the places where RELIGION comes into the methodology of Huna.

Now rest a few moments, turning off the recorder, then come back to it for some questions and answers.

* * * * * * * *

QUESTIONS AND ANSWERS

Q. Isn't the healing you have described the same old one of "Laying on Hands"?
A. It certainly IS, but in this case we learn from Huna what, besides making a prayer, we are to do in the ancient healing ritual. BUT, one does not have to touch the one treated after an aka or shadowy thread of contact is established. "Absent treatment" as practiced in the metaphysical cults of today makes good use of the aka threads without knowing that they are doing so. Look at a person, hear his voice, or see his picture or his signature written in ink, and your low self can pick up a thread and follow it in a flash to contact the Person.

Q. Did the Egyptians have a word for this kind of healing?
A. It is not known whether they did or not, but the kahuna initiates in later Hawaii had a fine code word to name and still conceal the meaning of the name of the process. They were great layers on of hands, and they called the hands *mana-mana*, which codes the fact that much mana went through the hands. The outer meaning of the word *mana-mana*, however, was "hands," or it meant "to divide"--the "dividing" being partly code in telling us that we shared our mana or divided it with the person treated.

Q. When the evangelist, Kathryn Kuhlman, heals people and makes them fall unconscious into the arms of the "catcher," is she using mana, perhaps a form of mesmeric shock?
A. From what we know of Huna, it seems probable that she is. In an audience where emotions run high, mana is automatically generated and can be picked up as a surcharge by a speaker. She probably causes enough mana to go into the person treated to enable the healing to be done by whatever agency may be at work. Unfortunately, when the mana charge is all used up, the low self of the one healed may cause the malady to return. If this happens, a second healing seems very difficult. Under ideal conditions, the treatment which results in an instant healing should be followed up with daily treatments with mana for several days.

Q. What is the difference between the three manas which are named as three elements in the composition of man?
A. It is not known whether there is a change in the nature of the low mana when

it is taken and used by either the middle or High Self. It has been spoken of as a change in voltage, but it seems most likely that the nature of the mana changes little or just a little, and that the difference lies in the USE made by a particular self of the basic life force. Mana is not like ordinary electricity which we use in the radio with variations in the frequency and pressure. In telepathy, for instance, the messages have been known to travel to the other side of the earth without weakening. If the mana was like the electricity in radio messages, these weaken with the increase in distance traveled.

Q. You said that the mana used by the High Self was symbolized as honey by the early Egyptians, and that the bee was its symbol. How about the low mana? Did they have a symbol for it also?
A. Yes. They had a very amusing symbol, the grasshopper. This insect symbolized the low self, and because it secreted a brown "tobacco" juice (as we called it when I was a boy) from its mouth, the juice was used as the symbol of the low mana made by the low self. Drawings of the grasshopper were also made and used with special significance by the early Egyptians.

Now, I wish you my aloha.

MFL

* * * * * * * * *

SHORT TALK ON HUNA

NUMBER FOUR

BY MAX FREEDOM LONG

GREETINGS!

THIS IS MAX FREEDOM LONG SPEAKING.

In our study of Huna, the ancient system of the SECRET, we are drawing our information from several sources. When I was a young man, I went to Hawaii and began to hear stories of what the kahunas were doing. I had majored in Psychology at school after becoming converted to Theosophy. But before that, as a high school student in a small Colorado town, I had taken a look at all the religions I could find listed in the Encyclopaedia.

Some of you may also have been brought up to accept one religion and to go to one church or synagogue--be told that it was a sin to disbelieve what you were taught. I happened to be a Baptist. That was just by chance. But I was also a boy given to much curiosity and THAT was something rather universal. Curiosity will kill the cat of a boy of any religion, be it one of the old and time-honored ones dating back to Moses, or one of the new religions of the New Thought school.

I wanted to know a lot of things. I wanted to know WHY the Baptists, to whom I belonged, were right and all the others wrong. I tried to talk to our preacher about my desire to know, and he was horrified. Everyone who was on the right side of the fence KNEW that we were right! I might just as well have questioned the existence of God and the fact that Jesus, who was to be anointed or "Christed" (from the Greek) and died on the cross to save man from the taint of original sin--the sin of Adam and Eve in the Garden--the sin that I never could understand WHY it should be visited on people of my later generation. Well, as you may guess, I got no change out of our Baptist Minister. He was greatly agitated and prayed for me to have faith.

I had equally bad luck with the Methodist and Presbyterian preachers. The Mormons were better in some ways. They were filled with zeal, but I couldn't accept Joseph Smith's tablets of gold which he translated by the use of two small stones--producing The Book of Mormon. I thanked my informant and bowed out. The Catholic Priest was best of all. He gave me a fine account of the Church from its inception, BUT ended by insisting that, as the Church had now given me the correct doctrine, I must join it or I would be LOST. I tried to argue, but to no avail. So I thanked him and went on my way.

I studied *Science and Health* and saw how all was unreal, but I was still unable to accept it. I still wanted to know why we must be saved from the sins of Adam. Then I chanced to meet a bewhiskered old Atheist and told him my trouble. He smiled and said, "My boy, you have run into the thing that all religion is based upon. You have run into the thing which has caused men to make war on one another for centuries. You have run into the thing which has caused men to become hermits, or to allow themselves to be broken on the wheel of the Inquisition rather than to change. You have run into DOGMA! Start looking for the dogmas upon which any religion is built, and you will then begin to understand how religions were put together. Some man--some fellow who is supposed to have a 'gift'--has a vision or an inspiration, or he makes up a yarn out of whole cloth. He tells it to people as the last word in TRUTH, and after a while they come to believe him. He has established his DOGMA. He proceeds to write a book. And anything that gets into a book is crystallized and becomes a TRUTH--or Dogma. Once it is accepted as a fact, you can count your religion all set. People begin to pass on the dogmas to their children, and it becomes a great sin to doubt the dogmas.

"The story of Adam and Eve and the Fall is a piece of Folklore. There are two main versions of it. But once it got into a book, it became God's own truth, and you denied it at the risk of being churched. Don't let anyone blinded by his own belief in a set of dogmas try to teach you. He can't see beyond his beliefs. Get into the source books and examine them. See for yourself what always happens--a belief or dogma is invented and accepted. It then is built on and built on and built on. Don't let anyone fool you, boy. It is ALL DOGMA and invention, and it is all man-made. No so-called 'revelation' will agree with any other 'revelation.' Don't accept any one of them."

I later came to think that Theosophy was rather logical in the belief in many incarnations, and in that respect, I became a Theosophist. But--to get back to my experience in Hawaii and the tales of what the kahunas were doing, let me continue.

I heard that they did a lot of magic, but most of all that in time just recently past, they had fire-walked on red-hot lava, as it overflowed from a volcano. I talked with two old Hawaiians who had seen it done. I didn't know it at the time, but at last I had run into something that may or may not have originated with a dogma, but which WORKED. I decided to look into the matter and eventually went to the curator of the Bishop Museum of Natural History in Honolulu and asked him whether or not there was any truth in the reported fire-walking.

His name was Dr. Brigham, and he was heavy with scientific honors--a great scientist--and he looked like Santa Claus. When he had heard me out, he said, "Yes, they used to do fire-walking in my early days here in Hawaii." He went on then to tell me how he had walked across red-hot lava and burned off his heavy mountain boots, while the old kahunas had crossed barefooted. No one was burned. No one had treated their feet with anything. All that the old natives did was to pray to "The Goddess of the Sky" for protection from the heat--and it was given.

NOW I was confronted by something which was NOT all dogma! Here was a very DIFFERENT thing. Here were native priests of a kind who prayed to some Higher Being, and who got results. I continued my questioning and learned that they also did remarkable HEALING.

"What have these people got?" I demanded.

Dr. Brigham said, "A system of

psychology and religion which is pure enough and close enough to its source--whatever that may have been--to work for them. If you want to study it and try to learn the secret behind what they did, always watch for three things: some unit of *CONSCIOUSNESS* guiding some unit of *FORCE,* and making it work through some form of *SUBSTANCE*. It will be very scientific when you find it. I have tried for forty years to find out how they do things, but the secret lore is very sacred to the native priests, or was before they died out under the impact of the modern civilization. They would not tell."

So, it came about that I started trying to learn the secret lore. Years passed before I found a code hidden in their language which told me what they believed and how they used it for healing--for fire-walking--for looking into the future to a certain extent--for slow healing and instant healing--and for several other things which we need not list here.

I realize that I am treading on many toes. Most of us have been born into dogmatic beliefs and have thoughtlessly accepted them as the one and only TRUE set of beliefs. The human animal has one strange characteristic: once he has taken a dogma to his heart, he ceases to be a man and becomes--at least in that respect--a MULE. He will balk at giving up a *DOGMA*. A mule has no sex, and this goes for the ladies as well as the men, even more so. They will refuse steadfastly to listen to all arguments against their beliefs, no matter how you approach them.

Dr. Brigham, as it eventually turned out, was not inclusive enough. He might have raised his sights or used a scatter-gun when he said we would have to watch for <u>consciousness</u> to work with a <u>force</u>, through a <u>substance</u>. We have in Huna THREE forms of consciousness, working with THREE forms of force, and using, in addition to the usual physical substance of the body, a strange and invisible substance--that of the three shadowy bodies of man. But of one thing he was correct in his anticipation: when we found these things, they would be "scientific." I grant you that the men of science have not yet quite caught up with these things, but they are of the kind science will acknowledge once it can get the tools to measure them. Scientists have to be able to measure everything, you know, or get it into a test tube.

The language CODE used by the Polynesians was preserved in the many, little islands of the Pacific for at least 2,000 years. We know this and set that length of time because they brought with them all the main stories which are found in the Bible. That is, in the Old Testament. They had the story of the Creation and of Adam and Eve and the Garden. They had a fine account of Noah and the Flood. They even had Jonah and the Whale. But, what they did NOT have was any trace of the story of Jesus or Mary or of the Crucifixion.

When the Missionaries arrived in Hawaii in 1820, they couldn't understand HOW the natives had come by the Old Testament stories, and finally decided that the Devil must have told them! It could not have been the earlier explorers, for if they had told of Adam and Eve, they certainly would have told of Jesus and his disciples. It is evident to us that they left the lands in or near Egypt at a time prior to the general knowledge of the Great Drama which was had in some way from the kahunas and mistaken for a real account of a real man.

The Egyptians, some long time before that, had preserved in their glyphs or picture-writing the information that they were "scientific" in that they, too, knew the three kinds of consciousness, three kinds of vital force (or mana), and the visible and invisible substance used by consciousness when working with the forces--the three shadowy bodies to match the three "selves" and their three "manas."

The picture-writing that has come down to us from the temples and tombs had already been evolved to the stage at which a single glyph stood for a letter, but to be sure the sentence would be understood, they put at the end of it a glyph which represented the main idea. You spelled out "mother" and then made a glyph picture of a woman to go with the spelled-out "mother." In this way, from their writing, we have the glyph as in the very ancient times, for the three selves or spirits of man. The bird has always been a code word for a spirit, and the stork in particular. So, we have in early Egypt three storks collapsed together to make almost one, but standing for the three UNITED selves of the man. For his mana, the code has always been "water." (Remember our grasshopper, who could produce water from its mouth when caught, and which was the symbol of the low or subconscious self?) This glyph was not of just one wavy line, but of THREE, one above the other. And for the three shadowy bodies of the man they used three umbrellas, one for each of the three selves.

The language code, when I discovered after years of work that there was one and began to try to break it, was a double code. For instance, they had a word for a normal ghost which meant a spirit of three waters. The "waters" meant that the ghost had all three of its manas, but it took me a very long time to find out what "waters" stood for. It was a code within a code. By the way, the kahunas had no written language in early Egypt. Nor is there any writing in the pyramids.

The Great Pyramid is supposed to have been built to serve as a tomb for a Pharaoh, but while contemporary tombs have much writing in them and burial furnishings, the interior seems to have been designed as a SYMBOL of the THREE SELVES. At the bottom of the structure and well below the ground surface, we find the "Well." It is a small chamber and is supposed to serve as a drainage sump. From it leading upward is a passage that connects with the Grand Gallery, which leads to the "King's Chamber" at the top. But half way up a second passage leads off to a smaller room known as the "Queen's Chamber" and which is just right for the middle self in this symbology. The largest room, which is reached by a very narrow opening at the end of the Grand Gallery, contains an open sarcophagus in which no body was ever placed. Well we may ask WHY? Did they symbolize the death and burial of the man as having something to do with his High Self? Was the spaciousness of the King's Chamber the silent evidence of the greater power and glory of the self called by the kahunas, "The Utterly Trustworthy Parental

Spirit"? Did the low-self room, buried deep in the rock beneath the pyramid show the hidden nature of the subconscious or low self? Did the larger chamber next above stand for the middle self? Did the passages leading always upward to the highest room stand for the aka cords that make the connection for us between the three selves?

In this great monument, we find no effort made to represent the three manas or vital forces, or to picture the shadowy substance. It might be that if we understood the symbology in the Grand Gallery, we would have these items back. But, given the three selves and the shadowy cords, we can guess at the rest.

From any point of view, the primary dogma of the High Self stands out here as the most logical and believable. It gives us God as something brought down to within our reach. Above the High Self there may be still higher and higher Beings, but for our purposes and for our immediate help, it is enough that we know that the High Self is there--that it is a PART of ourselves, and that it stands ready to help us whenever we learn to do our parts in the calling.

For centuries we have known dimly that there was a Higher Being. This is the basic and true dogma of religions. We have prayed to God under many names and in many languages, and all prayers have gone to the High Selves because there was no place else for them to go--no mechanism except the mana flow along the shadowy cord, carrying our thought-pictures. (The fervent FAITH has caused clear pictures of our needs to be made and we have believed that our prayers would be answered, in many cases, without knowing Huna.)

In the great Drama of Initiation we have the figure representing the High Self declaiming the Secret Lore. He says, "According to your FAITH, so shall it be unto you."

Men have prayed without faith and have received an answer which was made up of two parts--the picture of the need, and the picture of it continuing. These two pictures cancel each other and we get nothing. Or we get a little more or less of what we ask. Men have tried endlessly to explain this failure. They have made sacrifices of all kinds, but they have not known that what we must give as our offering is MANA. It is the mana we accumulate by breathing more deeply and by commanding our low selves to gather an extra charge. It is this mana which we consciously offer with the picture of the desired thing, or condition, to the High Self as our prayer. We furnish the thought-form-seed. We water it with mana (water is the code word for mana.) The High Self begins to materialize or grow the seed. Daily, in full confidence, we send mana and renew our picture. Then, one fine day the "ANSWER" suddenly is there.

Now for the discussions.

* * * * * * * *

QUESTIONS AND ANSWERS

In discussing the things of this short lecture, I suggest that you refer back to the earlier talks and be reminded of the Huna prayer methods.

Q. Was there not, a number of years ago, a PREDICTIVE system worked out by enthusiasts to show that the Great Pyramid was the embodiment of a prophesy of the "Last Days"?

A. Yes. What was called "the pyramid inch" was calculated and the Grand Gallery was measured inch by inch along the floor. Notches and markings along the Gallery were said to match events from the time of Jesus to the date of World War I, and its end was predicted by markings close to the opening of the passage into the King's Chamber. There was much speculation about what would happen as the inches were measured off along the chamber floor. Some said that when the inches (each inch at that point of measurement was supposed to represent a year) reached the sarcophagus,the Thousand Years of Peace under divine rule was expected. There might be a Christian "Second Coming," a Millenium.

There was a large book published giving all the measurements and charts and predictions. Behind the activity was a group of English people, and it became more or less a cult. I remember following the arguments and pouring over the book. I watched for the dates and....nothing happened. The years inched across the floor of the King's Chamber, and came to the back wall. Still nothing had happened but more wars. Some efforts were made to change the measurements a little, but that did not help. Little by little we gave up hoping. It had been a false dogma. The Great--the wonderful Pyramid--had let us down. Today the big book is a curiosity to be found only in used book stores or on the shelves of some misguided student who has ceased to hope.

Q. Is there any way to be sure that we have accumulated a charge of mana before we offer it as a sacrifice or gift to the High Self?

A. Yes, it was found that the pendulum would measure the size of the mana charge. If you are one of those who can use the pendulum, hold it over the palm of your left hand (if you are right-handed) and ask it to show you by a circular swing how much mana you have aboard. It will show by making a small circle with its swing. (You must remember that the low self is causing the pendulum to swing. A pendulum may be said to act as a means of communication between the low and middle self.) Now begin to breathe rhythmically in sets of four deeper and slower breaths, EXPECTING the low self to take on more mana by burning more blood sugar. It knows how if you set it to work. After about four sets of four breaths, take up your pendulum and ask again for the measurement of the mana charge. In most cases you will find the circle made by the swinging pendulum very much larger. Offer the mana to the High Self and send with it the mental picture of the thing for which you wish to pray--as if you had already been given it. Give thanks that your prayer is being materialized by the High Self and that the "seed" has sprouted and has started to grow. After you have finished and broken off your prayer/action, take up your pendulum and measure yourself again for the mana charge. You will find that it is all expended or you may be able to get no measurement at all and the pendulum will hang quietly, not moving. You will, of course, quickly build up your mana charge again, or you can breathe a few times and charge up to your normal level. Try this. It will give you faith in the method. MFL.

SHORT TALK ON HUNA

NUMBER FIVE

BY MAX FREEDOM LONG

GREETINGS!

This is Max Freedom Long speaking again.

As you will remember, we started out to discuss the TEN ELEMENTS in the ancient Huna system. These are the three selves or spirits which make up the man; the three grades of mana or vital force used by the three selves; and the three shadowy or *aka* bodies which are invisible but which play a large part in our lives. Finally, we have the physical body while we are alive on this level of existence.

For the moment, let us consider the shadowy bodies. That of the low or subconscious self is a most amazing thing. It is an exact duplicate of every tissue, bone and organ of the body. It seems to be a form of mold, and to be all but indestructible.

The English and American Societies for Psychical Research have run down all the ghost stories. They have reported many psychic experiments on the parts of their members down the years. They have given us excellent evidence of the various kinds of psychical experience, but they have never been able to work out an answer to the problems they have raised. Today the American

Society is fifty years behind the times and makes little progress. The Huna explanations are rejected. They will not even consider them, and without them, they have not a single explanation for their findings which will hold water.

Let us see what problems are left unsolved by the SPR in one of the most interesting cases recorded in Nandor Fodor's *Encyclopaedia of Psychic Science*. Pages 243-244. Carlo Mirabelli was born of Italian parentage in 1889 in São Paulo, Brazil. When he first began to show signs of his mediumship, no one near him knew what to make of it. They had hardly heard of Spiritualism. In fact, they decided that he needed to be placed in an asylum by the police and others. But soon he was brought to the attention of more knowledgeable men and his activities were most carefully studied and reported on in several languages. The things that he did are perhaps the best certified in the history of investigations by the Psychical Researchers.

What got him into the asylum until a newspaper brought pressure to bear to get him out was his "levitation" and his "transportation." He would be standing with his friends and suddenly would vanish--only to turn up at a railroad station 90 kilometers distant. He would float in the air above the heads of his friends as they walked down the street.

Let us pause to ask how he could become invisible, clothing and all, at a moment's notice, and wire back from the distant railway station only minutes later. What became of his body? When it became changed by what is agreed upon were spirit or other supernormal forces, WHY didn't the material of his body and clothing just fall apart and never be collected again? Huna gives us the shadowy body as the answer. It is, as I said, a MOLD of every part of the body, and when the body is changed to what is called "invisible ectoplasm" by the spirits, the shadowy bodies are left intact. They then are as light as a *thought*. They can be transported to a distance, and can there be made solid again--"materialized." The clothing was also handled in the same way, and we must say that it had an aka or shadowy counterpart that held together and could be dematerialized and then materialized. And, by the way, that is the best explanation yet offered for HOW flying saucers get to earth from very distant planets, and suddenly appear and fly around, as suddenly disappearing. It is the "mat and demat" theory proposed first by Meade Layne of California. So far it is the ONLY explanation that will account for their arrival here and for their activities. To go in the form of a physical Saucer from some far planet to planet Earth AT THE SPEED OF LIGHT would take a lifetime--many of them--to get to the nearest probable visiting point. BUT, if they can be, by some use of FORCE by some INTELLIGENT BEINGS made to "demat,' then to go at the speed of THOUGHT, they would get there quickly and could "mat" up to physical solidarity, investigate, do whatever Flying Saucer Beings come to do, and, "demat," and go home. Light is the fastest thing we know, but consider a distance of a few "light years," and you will see how necessary it would be to get into another level of material, if not of consciousness, for such trips.

Well, Carlos Mirabelli was no saucer

man, but he could go places and do things on the instant. Incidentally, other mediums were transported from place to place in a moment of time. Apports are thus brought to the seance room. Just because you may not have happened to have heard of these things of Psychical Research is no reason why you should deny them. Bear with me for the time being, and later on go read up on what I am talking about. Don't be like my late brother-in-law who died and as a spirit was found by a spirit friend of mine and asked to come back to earth and talk with me as I sat in a seance. He refused to come, saying, "I don't believe in ghosts." And if you are one who can't swallow the ghost or other theories, try to accept them as a possibility and hear me out.

In broad daylight, being watched by investigators, Mirabelli often caused dead people to return and materialize so fully that doctors investigated them, took their temperature, listened to their heart and pronounced them to be normal living men in all ways. One of these was Dr. Jose de Carmago Barros, so he said. He had lived some time ago and had lost his life in a shipwreck. He had been a bishop. Dr. Fodor describes it thus:

"A sweet smell of roses filled the room. The medium went into a trance. A fine mist was seen in the circle. The mist, glowing as if of gold, parted and the bishop materialized, with all his robes and insignia of office. He called his own name. Dr. de Souza stepped to him. He palpated the body, touched his teeth, tested his saliva, listened to his heart-beat, investigated the working of the intestines, nails and eyes, without finding anything amiss. The other attending persons convinced themselves of the reality of the apparition. The Bishop smilingly bent over Mirabelli and looked at him silently. Then he slowly dematerialized."

How does the SPR explain these things? It does not. It cannot. Huna, however, gives us a logical and direct picture of the mechanism. Forces are used of which we know little, but in the hands of the right intelligences they can FILL the surviving SHADOWY BODIES of people like the Bishop. To do this they must control heat and cold, and in bringing apported objects they do this. But the shadowy bodies are the thing. They are lived in after death, and they survive for a long time. In her book, *Winged Pharaoh*, Joan Grant goes back to early Egypt and tells of her experience as a woman of that time. She has reincarnated many times since, but the MEMORY is retained, and the shadowy bodies are passed on from one incarnation to the next. A different body in a different time and place--same shadowy body. We are immortal in our shadow body and the bodily substance that fills them is changed, but the SELVES return to make use of the new bodies. We rest between incarnations and absorb the lessons we have learned from each life's experience.

There is a certain amount of heat generated in changing matter from the solid form to the invisible form. This is controlled by the spirits or other high entities (we postulate the High Self as the one actually able to handle mat and demat, but there may be similar spirits of a high order who are not human--Nature Spirits, if you will). We see the fire-walkers making their appeal to several different Entities, the Polynesian one simply being called "Lady of the Sky," but the Goddess Mariana is appealed to by the men of India who fire-walk in Fiji, their adopted country.

Apports include all sorts of things in all kinds of condition. Mirabelli brought across apports of human beings, you might say, as well as of many other kinds. In England, at seances, such things as gems and ancient Roman coins were brought. In one seance a pan of frying eggs was brought, sizzling hot. Later a block of ice with a fish frozen in it came. Flowers are frequent apports, and often they arrive wet, the spirits saying that they were wet to protect them from the heat of transit. Growing plants in pots have arrived, and plant growth has been stimulated greatly, as in cases in which seeds were planted, a whole orange tree made to grow in a matter of minutes and to produce fruit.

Healing belongs in this category. Some mediums have spirit friends who work through them, using the same methods to bring about healing. The best of them can mat and demat in treating tumors and growths. Recently there has been a furor over the several Spiritistas in the Philippines who have done this work. Openings have been made in the abdomen and growths taken out, then the opening closed instantly, leaving no scar. An amusing thing happened to one healer. He was arrested for practicing medicine without a license and accused of removing a growth. The man who had been operated upon had been rounded up and put on the stand. He admitted that he had been opened and that a ball of something had been removed. But when asked to show his scar, he could show nothing at all. The judge dismissed the charges.

In one seance in England which was

attended by newspaper reporters bent on investigating the reports of the materialization of animals, the spirit seems to have been playful. It did not bring the usual pets to greet their former masters who sat around the table. Instead, they brought a bear and it was not friendly. The reporters fled in dismay. They had all the investigating they wanted.

The shadowy bodies have another strange characteristic. They can be made large or small. Very small materializations of people have been observed, perfect in most respects, but very small, say a foot in height.

It would be unfair to Mirabelli to leave him without recounting some of his other mediumistic feats. When being investigated in Italy under test conditions, he spoke in twenty-six languages including seven dialects. He wrote in twenty-eight languages, including Latin and Chaldaic and Hieroglyphics. Of the sixty-three tests, forty were made in daylight, twenty-three in bright artificial light, for, unlike many mediums, he worked openly and without a darkened room. In his writing he did automatic writing, producing messages from many dead celebrities, including fourteen pages in nineteen minutes in French, and five pages in twelve minutes in Japanese on the Russo-Japanese war under control of Muri Ka Ksi. Moses wrote through him in Hebrew on slandering. A Catholic priest was so impressed by the things done that he left the Church and wrote a book about it. He is not long gone, and I had a letter recently from a woman who was sitting with a group, hoping to get similar psychic phenomena. I have the book someplace on my shelves. I have forgotten the exact title, but the author is (Ex)-Father Greber, as I recall. (Johannes Greber, *Communications With the Spirit World*, 1932).

There is so much that we do not know. The Egyptians may have understood just how the spirits manipulated substance to make it into its invisible form, or they may not. Whether the later initiates knew or not, or whether the kahunas when they got to Polynesia retained a knowledge of the intricate mechanisms of the *aka* or shadowy bodies, we may never know. For instance, we look at a child and wonder. It may have incarnated in its ancient Egyptian shadowy body, but what have the genes of the Western parents done in filling the aka body? The Egyptians were dark people. This child is light? All we can do is speculate that with the material furnished by the mother, the body is built, and it may vary from one race to another. I will not worry the question, but it is left wide open. Perhaps some future investigator will find the answer. But one thing we do know, and that is that in certain cases, when memories are brought over from the far past, they belong to something that lasts and lasts and lasts. It may well be that the low self can work and live with bodily materials of various sorts--a mixture from both father and mother--and still retain its INDIVIDUALITY.

The shadowy body of the middle self seems to have evolved a step from the animal world to which the low self belongs. It is said to be of a finer texture, and to house the middle-self spirit of man as he uses his reason--which is his great gift, along with SPEECH.

The shadowy body of the High Self is

of still finer material. It is a step from being nothing at all, one might say. It seems to be able to glow with light with great ease, and may be of the nature of light, which is its symbol.

This lovely symbol got into the practices of the churches in some way. The Hebrews had a candlestick made of gold as part of the sacred furniture of the Ark of the Covenant, so we read. In the Four Gospels, which were written as a drama to be played and used in initiating the kahunas of that day, the symbol is stressed. The lead character in the drama says, "I am the Light of the world; he who walketh after my way will not walk in darkness." Jesus was playing the part of the High Self. And later, still as the High Self, he said, "I am the Way, and the Life," which codes for us the High Self. In China we find the candle in the temples where almost all of the original Huna lore has been lost, and in the Catholic churches around the world we find candles lighting the altars, and being burned to the further glory of Mary or a favorite saint.

In daytime the Sun was the symbol. It was "Ra" in Egypt, and became changed to "La" in Hawaii for they had no letter "r" as the Missionaries wrote the language to fit the sounds. By night there was the candle, and in some rites the candle or fire is kept constantly burning as a reminder of the greatness and glory of the *Aumakua* or "Utterly Trustworthy Parental Spirit." This self, by the way, has a great lore surrounding it. In passing let me say only that in it the male and female who were separated and are symbolized by Adam and Eve are once more united. Their powers are thus doubled. But they remain the loving parents watching over the low and middle selves as they live and learn and evolve upward.

The prayers we make are best when done after the Huna fashion, sending the thought-forms of the perfect state or condition on a flow of mana across the shadowy cord. We consciously generate that extra mana to send, asking the low self to help us. There are Laws of which we wot not in this universe, and we pray right to be right under the Law that governs our intercourse with the High Self.

Now for the Question and Answer period.

* * * * * * * *

QUESTIONS AND ANSWERS

Q. Did Mirabelli see into the future as one of his accomplishments?

A. In the recorded accounts of his work there is no mention of pre-vision on his part. This seems to be a gift that comes by itself as a rule, seldom with other mediumistic talents.

The Huna theory is that the High Self is the only one able to see what is being made for the future, and events are said to be built first into *aka* or shadowy bodies which match them. As the time arrives, the event in its physical form is materialized. For each of us the High Self is said to grow shadowy bodies of our future, building into it the things we send it. All day we hope and fear and even if we do not know it, the thoughts are taken by the High

Selves and used to build into our FUTURE.

To change the future which we have helped build hit-and-miss in this way, from a mixed and muddled set of arriving events to those which we desire, we have to begin to send daily, or hourly in cases of emergency, the mental pictures of the desired conditions, be these of health, or corrected relations with friends, finances, inner awakening to spiritual truths--our needs are many.

Phineus P. Quimby, the forerunner of New Thought, was a mesmerist in New England in the past century. He was also a healer, and he discovered that when he made the healing pictures for a person, they often had two or three days in which they were decidedly worse. But if they kept expecting the improvement which he promised them, in a few days they began to get better.

In putting Huna to work we have noticed the same thing. It is as if the High Self had to break up the shadowy body of the bad things already created for us, and then to replace them with the new picture. Often it seems as if the worst was about to befall, but the "Storm is tempered to the lamb," and if we hold the faith and keep sending the correct pictures to the High Self, things begin to improve. In the Old Testament, Job is the classic example of a man who learned this lesson. He came to the point where he said that even if God slew him, still would he trust. It is a good example for us. If we will give up hating, clean house as best we can, and do a few things to make our low self feel that we DESERVE being helped, then make and send the pictures of what we desire to the High Self, we will, within reason, get them.

Often we find that if we have two or three friends who will join us in making the Huna prayers for the desired condition, it helps. Jesus, speaking as the High Self, said, "When two or three are gathered in my name, ..." The additional mana that is sent helps greatly, and the friends can make a picture less apt to be tainted by the realization of the bad or present conditions. Generate all the EMOTION you can in DESIRING the changed condition. The low self is the one who makes the emotions, and if you can desire greatly and fervently, you will know the low self is helping with the prayer. A "cold" prayer is a middle-self reasoning action, but add the work of the low self and it becomes a "warm" and living prayer.

Q. What is an "unreasonable prayer"--a request for too much?

A. One must use common sense and not ask for the moon, but above all do not ask the High Self to take something away from the other fellow and give it to you. It won't "rob Peter to pay Paul" for you, and it won't force anyone to do something against his will. Ask for help in getting something, and leave it to the High Self to find that help for you. It may take time, if what you ask is difficult. Keep asking.

And again my aloha,

MFL.

SHORT TALK ON HUNA

NUMBER SIX

BY MAX FREEDOM LONG

GREETINGS!

Your speaker again is Max Freedom Long.

The question has been asked for centuries, "Where are the memories of past lives stored that they may be carried over from one life to another?"

The founder of the Theosophical Society, Mme. Helena Blavatsky, was a Russian woman of good birth who was married at the age of eighteen to an old general, whom she left at once and set off to study the religions of Tibet and India. She was well equipped for this, being a natural medium and psychic, and able to grasp the abstractions of the religions of these two ancient lands.

After getting all she could out of the Tibetan wise men, she went to India and began sorting the several hundred cult beliefs, taking from each a little, and in due time, she came up with a fairly straight line of beliefs dating back to the original Vedas and the Sanskrit-speaking days. This she carefully set down in books and it was not long before the Western world began to ready what she had written; also to understand the religious concepts of Yoga, the Vedas and much that she tried to fill in and make reasonable.

Among the things which she unearthed was the very old belief that there were seven "bodies of man." This was almost a full recovery of Huna and its TEN ELEMENTS OF MAN, including a double of the body, but missing the High Self and its shadowy body. It is now evident that there was an intercourse with the original KAHUNAS sometime in the very formative days of the Vedas, but that, as time passed, the lore was distorted and partly lost.

To tell the truth, Blavatsky was a little vague about these "bodies," and when her younger friend, Annie Besant, came to take over a part of the Society and to start her own writing in an endeavor to make clear the earlier and more ponderous writings of the Madame, the explanations she gave still lacked considerable. She mixed the shadowy bodies with the elements of the three selves, giving us an "emotional body" for the low-self aka body. Then there was a "Mental body" for the middle self or conscious mind's shadowy body.

When it came to naming the three vital forces or manas of the man, one frequency for each of the three selves, she was especially flustered. It so happened that in Sanskrit the word "mind" happened to be *manas*, so you couldn't use mana in that language for vital force, and the early men of India had used the word, *prana*, for a substitute. They knew that there was more than one kind of this force, and took to speculating about it. Everything has its own mana to hold it together and make it alive, and for man they soon had several manas or *pranas*, one for thinking with, one for feeling emoticns, one for this and that. As years rolled on, the Secret was lost and they added dozens of *pranas*, one for almost anything a man could imagine himself doing.

For the three selves they gradually lost the Huna concept and decided to settle for two: one included the low self and the middle, the other vaguely covered the High Self. But they had, however, the "monad" or a unit of "self" that was the forerunner of the High Self--perhaps a level above it in the scale of existence. It was the "divine spark" that gives life and form and consciousness and is more like what we postulate as a "Nature Spirit" presiding over vegetable and animal forms and keeping everything working under the LAW. This monad also came down a step and incarnated in man as the Atma-Buddhi-Manas, which covers roughly the SELVES of Huna.

As there may be a learned Theosophist listening, and who may take issue with what I have said, let me set all right by quoting from Hoult's *Dictionary of Theosophical Terms*, p. 126, under the heading of "Seven Principles of Man." He writes:

"In the earlier writings of the Theosophical Movement these principles were referred to as (1) Atma, Spirit; (2) Buddhi, spiritual soul; (3) Manas, mind; (4) Kama, feeling; (5) Prana, life; (6) Linga-sharira, the etheric double; and (7) Sthula-sharira, the physical body. But there is confusion between 'bodies' and 'principles,' between the objective and the subjective, and it would appear that it is the five-fold universe--not the sevenfold--that man, as thus described, is related. The analysis is by no means satisfactory.

"Objectively considered, man is, perhaps, best described as consisting of a Mental Body (Causal and Manasic), an Astral Body, and a Physical Body (Dense and Etheric). These correspond with, and are in relation to, 'the three worlds;' and it is through, or by means of, these bodies that the 'Principles,' the

Jivatmic expression, manifest themselves. Higher than these three worlds, existence is arupa or formless, and the 'Principles' are Divine rather than human."

So, you see, it takes a little understanding of Huna to put things straight. And that brings us back to our original question of where man kept his memories between incarnations when he had no physical body.

The kahunas say in the shadowy body of the low or subconscious self. This body is, as I was at pains to explain in my last talk, PRACTICALLY INDESTRUCTIBLE. In it are stored the memories of many lives, but as we have no associated thoughts to help us to recall past lives, we seldom can relive them. But the THREE SELVES have, in some way, access to these memories, and can LEARN. If you are an old soul, or one who has lived several times, there are certain things which you automatically KNOW. We tend to avoid making the same very large mistake again and again and again. That is why people are so different. They have had different experiences and they will react differently in a similar situation according to their automatically recalled inner experience. The young soul is given to letting his emotions run away with him. Emotions are the things made for us by the low self, and are of the animal man. As we grow older in terms of incarnations, we tend to CONTROL OUR EMOTIONS instead of letting them control us. The young soul loves to fly into a rage when crossed. The old one endures in silence. BUT, there is one emotion which we do not live down, and that is LOVE. Instead, we learn to refine it as we grow. It is the great common denominator of growth. A perfect capacity to love marks the advanced soul. Eventually we learn to love well enough to be joined and blended with the intended mate--the Adam or Eve of the veiled mystery--and graduate to the High Self level. (I discuss this at much length in my book, *The Huna Code in Religions*.)

The kahunas taught that the only sin was that of hurting another. Nothing else one might do counted. Their belief might be reduced to a slogan: "NO HURT: NO SIN." This is a most inclusive doctrine and is the negative side of the command to stop hurting and LOVE. In religions the priests have laid a vast burden of SINS on the people. They found a fine target in sex, and in Christianity, whose dogmas were almost entirely formed by Paul, we find sex condemned as a great sin. He also invented the dogma that Jesus was crucified to save the world from the original sin of Adam and Eve, which mankind had never outlived. These things were most unreasonable and illogical, but they were largely what the Christian Church was built upon. Men and women became hermits to avoid sex. Women became nuns, and men became monks. Their priests were celibate. But Jesus didn't instruct them to avoid sex at all costs, and the reason he was not married is because, as a High Self, he was already united in the "marriage made in Heaven" to his own Eve.

But to get back to the shadowy body of the low self as the place in which the memories of other lives are stored to bring them across with us. It must be remembered that "thoughts are things" and that when we think them, the low self makes a tiny impression in the shadowy substance in some way, and stores it in its memory collection.

It may be likened to a tape on which sounds are recorded. Each memory has a place on the tape--a place in time--and if you set the low self hunting for a name you can't recall, it will, so to speak, run its tape, for the time and place where the person was met, and in due time will come up with the name. As we move out of past incarnations into the present, we lose the time and place part of the tape so that we have little to go on when we try to remember back so far.

In recent days we have had hypnotic regression into other lives, and a number of people have tried to go back for clients and see what they did and give them a "life reading"--usually not very accurate, I fear. In any case, the evidence is gradually mounting to show that some people DO recall naturally under hypnosis, their past lives. These recollections are usually very disconnected and vague, but often a life just lived will be recalled, and things we feared in that life, will be found to be causing our low selves to visit on us various mysterious ills.

Geraldine Cummings, a good medium, writes in one of her books of going back into the past life of a man who had a fixation and couldn't bring himself to sign papers of any kind. She saw that in the life just ahead he had had his hands cut off in connection with signing papers, and had carried over the fears. Once he understood this, he overcame his fears--drained off his complex, we say.

In a book by Joan Grant and Denys Kelsey, *Many Lifetimes*, Dr. Kelsey, who is a psychiatrist, throws much light on the fact that consciousness resides in the shadowy bodies of the united low and middle selves both in and between incarnations. In treating patients with mysterious physical or mental ills, he has often used hypnosis and caused them to go back, searching for lost memories of childhood, babyhood, and life before being born.

One of the most interesting cases which he describes had particular bearing on what we are discussing. There was a young woman who had a bad "rejection" complex. It did things to her health and kept her unhappy, even though married and with two children. He regressed her back to the time when she was conceived, even a bit before conception, and the memories of her sensations as an egg in the womb were clear and vivid. She described herself as a "spot" there and her deep feeling that she must NOT touch something else (the sperm) that was near--but touch it she did, and impregnation resulted. Later investigation turned up the fact that HER mother had been greatly afraid of having a baby and had tried to avoid it, this mental state seeming to affect the daughter who must have been hanging around in her shadowy bodies wanting to get a new body and incarnating again. The memory was there of the fact that she should not do it, but she did, and suffered all down the line thereafter with the feeling of not being wanted, as, indeed, she was not. But, once she understood the source of the trouble, she got rid of the fixation and began to enjoy her love of husband and children in a normal way. Get the book and read it, so that you can see for yourself. It may be on the news stands as a paperback by now. In it Joan Grant also tells of her natural ability to recall past lives, and recounts some of the far past experiences. She is famous for her book, *The Winged Pharaoh,* in which she went all the way back to the time of King Tut in Egypt. She might be called an expert in such matters and her comments carry some weight in our considerations.

In her book she makes a statement which will bear measure from the Huna point of view. Let me read to you from page two.

"By this time I had acquired sufficient empirical experience to see the broad outlines of the progress of an individual during the initial four phases of his evolution. He starts with only enough energy to organize a single molecule. As energy increases, and his consciousness begins to expand, he requires more complex forms through which to express them. After growing too adult to be contained in the mineral phase of existence, he enters the vegetable kingdom, and then graduates, by a series of incarnations as various species of animal, to his first incarnation as a member of the race of homo-sapiens.

"During his first few lifetimes as a human-being the whole personality incarnates, so he is likely to have approximately the same capacities and perceptions whether he happens to be incarnate or excarnate. But as his consciousness expands, it becomes too wide to be contained within the framework of a single personality. So the incarnate individual is now both a single personality and an integrated component of his total self."

We agree with the first part. It is reasonable and fits the Huna idea of evolution. But her last statement needs explaining, and she leaves the question there. Is she speaking of "integrating" what we call the three selves? (For what else is there to "integrate"?) Or has she something else in mind? But she gives a good general idea of what we live through as we come along in evolving up to the human stage. According to Huna, it joins a middle self at this point, and they go on together. This makes the animal or low self a companion to a more evolved self, and together they double their mental capacity, learn to talk and to use the higher or inductive type of reason. Over all of this growth the High Self is acting as the guide and director. It is the Self which has evolved a step beyond the middle self, and stands in the place of the Father and Mother combined.

It watches over us, never encroaching on our free will, and helping us as it watches us gain experience and grow in many ways. One of the ways in which we grow is in the accumulation of such experience as may teach us to be good and helpful and to LOVE more selflessly. We love because we understand. We understand what makes the less evolved people act like animals, grasping and greedy.

Behind each of us lies our <u>CONSCIENCE</u>. This is something of which we of the more evolved sort accept and understand. It is something within us that suffers guilt pangs if we do something unjust or refuse help where we might easily give it--if we do or do not do a thousand things.

Just what IS conscience? we may ask. The answer may well be that it is the unrecognized memories of all past experiences, the experiences of many incarnations. We do not have the ability to look back into earlier lives, but when confronted by a situation, we subconsciously recall what happened when we hurt another and later learned the hard way not to do it again. Sympathy and imagination unite in this background of knowledge, and indeed, it is the only knowledge granted to us that really counts.

Like Napoleon, when he had conquered Egypt and went to stand before the Great Pyramid and the Sphinx, saying, "Five thousand years look down upon us," WE stand with <u>such consciences</u> as we have developed and may say, "Five thousand years of life and experience are now breathing down my neck every time I am tempted to do something that is not worthy of the best that is in me."

Remember as you go along to avoid hurting others, and such other things as you may have done that you consider "sinful" will be forgiven you. Strive to learn to LOVE more fully, more expertly, for <u>there</u> is the <u>way out</u>.

* * * * * * * *

QUESTIONS AND ANSWERS

Q. How do you explain the fact that some people seem not to have a conscience, but take a fine delight in cheating and hurting others?

A. These are the late arrivals on the scene or they are those who have not yet learned that in the long run it does not pay to take advantage of others. There is a built-in justice which will eventually catch up with them.

Q. Why does God allow some to impose on others and let them "flourish as the green bay tree" and never seem to have to pay up?

A. In living as a low self in the <u>animal</u>

body, the theory is that we are subject to all the accidental difficulties of the animal level. God is supposed NOT to send diseases and plagues and poverty and sickness, but who knows what God is or wants? We seem to exist under some set LAW of growth and being, and as middle selves we share the trials and tribulations of the physical body. As fish or bird we may be eaten by some larger and stronger beast. As a man in a physical body we may be subjust to hurts done to us by the strong and ruthless. But we do not die. We go to the other side for a while and rest up, absorb the lessons we have learned, and then return to incarnate once more. What looks like rank injustice to us may be just NECESSITY under some great Law which guides all of evolution. (Or can you think of a better answer?)

Q. Where and when and how does this train of evolution end?

A. The traditions of religion vary, and aside from them, we have little to guide us in the matter. The Vedic lore of India teaches that there is a great outpouring that goes on for a long cycle, then comes a turn in the opposite direction and the outgoing becomes the ingoing as each cycle ends. Between cycles there are periods of rest. This is reincarnation on a world scale, you will notice. We blow up our short lives and incarnations to world size in time and space.

In the Bible we have a more materialistic approach and read of the Day of Judgment. The subject has held the fascinated attention of true believers for many years, and they have combed the Prophesies looking for signs that the Last Day was around the corner. Some have thought that they had even the date figured out, and I remember as a child the rumor that had circulated giving a certain day and hour for the great event. I heard the elders talking in hushed voices about it, and was not at all certain what might happen. I prayed twice as loud and long on the eve of the Day, and ...awoke in the morning delighted to find myself safe.

Be that as it may, the Indian concept may be closer to the truth. We are asked to believe by some that the fabled Atlantis rose to be a great civilization, then destroyed itself--leaving the world populated by a few pockets of isolated people who began all over from scratch. It is an interesting speculation that makes us wonder if we are not drawing to a close of an age. Mathematically, we have in incarnation about as many souls as there may be in existence, and with the population explosion threatening in another few years all by itself to exterminate the human race, that might be one way out. Then there is the threat of an atomic war which might break out at any moment and exterminate all life with radiation. What Divine Power would be watching as the last act was staged, no one knows. If we are judged, no one knows by what standards, or do we know what will become of the selves in their shadowy bodies. The world will not be fit for habitation again until the radiation wears itself out, and so, what the Vedas speak of as the "Long Night" may follow. We may all rest and try again, or just rest. Meantime, we do well to do the best we can while there is time left, and try NOT TO HURT OTHERS, but LOVE THEM.

Aloha. MFL.

SHORT TALK ON HUNA

NUMBER SEVEN

BY MAX FREEDOM LONG

GREETINGS!

This is Max Freedom Long once more coming via tape to tell you about the ancient Egyptian system which had no name, but was call "The SECRET," or Huna, to use the language which was made especially to contain the lore, name its elements, and serve as a secret code to shield it from outsiders. This language was beautifully constructed, and served its purpose well. In it the Four Gospels were originally written, then translated into another language, probably Greek, as it was the current, official language of the time in the Holy Land.

We know that the Egyptians and the Greeks both had elaborate Mystery Plays which were used in the teaching and initiation of members, but there is no evidence to show that these plays were used in the lands where the Four Gospels, or four versions of the same Mystery Play were written.

It is evident that the Hebrews carried Huna with them when they left Egypt, and we find the code symbols used to cover up references to the ancient system in the Old Testament. Isaiah is a good place to dig for secret bits of coded Huna. Genesis, of course, started the ball rolling with the legend of the Creation and of the separation of the sexes to give us man and woman, Adam and Eve. The sexes, by the way, are said in the Secret to reunite at the end of a period of evolutionary growth and in doing so, to graduate from the lower to a higher level of being. On the higher level they become the Superconscious or High Self, the *Aumakua*, which word is filled with root meanings, one of which is "Time Parents," or the ones who have lived longest. They are the "Utterly Trustworthy Parental Pair," and stand over a dual pair of men and women as Guides or Guardian Angels. These are dual, because each man and woman is made up of a low or subconscious self, and a conscious or middle self. These various secret bits of knowledge have crept out into the religions of the uninitiated and have been misunderstood and warped out of shape. They were a little too advanced and complicated for the average run of undeveloped mortals in their beginning incarnations, and had to be made over to fit their need for something material to believe in.

For instance, take the usual concept of a god. To the savage mind all the different branches of THINGS were ruled over by "gods." They had a god of the storm, of the rain and of the lightning. These were what may be called High Selves or still Higher Beings, Nature Spirits, if you please. They actually were in some way connected with these things and had power over them. They stood over many things, creatures and animals as the High Selves stand over man, and if properly appealed to, could influence their charges for the benefit or whim of men. I have already mentioned in my talks the "calling of the sharks and turtles," in which a ritual invocation was chanted in Samoa, even by children, and the sharks and turtles in the sea made to gather at the base of a cliff above the ocean. Fire-walking is another example of being able to call on them for help in crossing hot coals or stones. Winds can be made to blow stronger or to be quiet, and it was said in the legends of the Polynesians that the earliest members of what was later to be called Polynesian peoples were able to make the winds blow just right to drive their great, double canoes day after day until they reached their "Promised Land"--Hawaii. They came from *Hawaiiki*, so the legends say, or the "Land of the Life-giving Dew," which no one knows as a definite place, but is thought by some to be here, or others, there. The word is part of the secret code, and really refers to the land in which they learned to breathe in deeply in sets of four deep breaths, accumulating mana as they did so, for the root *wai* in *Hawaiiki* means water--and water is the symbol of mana. This, then, when sent across or along the shadowy cord of connection to the High Self, gets the mana changed to a stronger kind and returned as the "Life-giving Dew" of healing. Or, it may cause the High Self to give us KNOWLEDGE, "clear seeing."

This is the HA RITE which is so stressed in the Four Gospels as the big and important thing that the leading character in the Drama, Jesus, was teaching.

The Nature Spirits were materialistic and served as the many gods worshiped by the uninitiated. The tribes related themselves to one of these Nature Gods, and over the world we find totem spirits of this kind appealed to and giving help.

For the more advanced, or initiate members of the human race, there was reserved a knowledge of the High Self. In Genesis we read, "Let US create man," the US showing the outer belief in which there were many gods. But the idea of the one or single God followed. It may have been a concept which escaped from the initiate kahunas ("Keepers of the Secret"). It grew to include all gods and Higher Beings, but lost any description of them. In this loss the idea became so vague that it hardly served the desire for something which could be imagined and pictured. The people needed a material God--something near and hovering and kind--who might be appealed to for help.

In answer to this need, there developed the belief in world saviors, and in these the people had what they needed and could understand. Jesus as a High Self in the Gospel Drama was not such a savior, so Paul made him one--after which all was well for some 2,000 years with Christians. And someone even closer and more understanding was Mary, the mother of Jesus. Or, there were Saints no end. In India, China and Japan Gautama Buddha, who taught no such thing, became the object of veneration as the Amada Buddha whose "heart doctrine" was that of a savior. One lived the best one could, and depended on the love of this savior to do what was needed to bring one to an escape from the wheel of reincarnation. We, who know Huna, see that his secret teaching was an escape from the middle-self level by graduating into that of the High Self--the only Nirvana possible.

In between the Nature Spirits as lesser gods, and the God which was postulated as all inclusive and one alone--who ruled the Universie out to the farthest star--we have in Huna a very modest concept. It gives us the High Self, just above us, and still higher lies the *akua aumakua*, or god-like Higher Selves, and above them, while there are supposed to range layer on layer of ever increasing growth, we know little, and we are unable to grasp their verity. In addition to the High Selves we have them as a united or group order, the "Great Company of Aumakuas." There are groups of which we know little, but may preside over certain groups of people, and the idea seems hardly enough to cover a whole nation. Again, we are faced with the familiar limitation of middle-self thinking.

The High Self follows the Law in that it cares for its children. In the creature world, the more evolved a creature becomes, the better it loves and cares for its offspring. Man cares most, and his children are longest of all in growing to maturity and being able to care for themselves. We learn to love after a selfish and very personal fashion in bringing children into the world and caring for them. But as High Selves the love becomes perfected and selfless, as does the love of the man and woman, who unite and blend their being as they graduate into a new High Self. This is the second great teaching of the Four Gospels. It is the "marriage made in Heaven," and to gain it we have to learn to love more perfectly.

During past incarnations, so we gather, the true mates are born in the same group at about the same time so that they can meet each other and continue the task of learning to love more perfectly. We seem to come back as wife and husband or as members of the same family, or as lovers. We have to overcome such things as sex rivalry--which causes the "war between the sexes"--and is really the instinctive effort of the couple to break down the differences between them and to get ready to blend and make a High Self. We try desperately to make the mate over and to make him or her conform to the ideal. In doing so we cause much trouble. The constant nagging of the wife may be such a reaction which has become chronic with her. The neglect and lack of love and tenderness on the part of the man may keep him from filling her innermost dream of the way he should be in the end.

One of our most important jobs is to learn to love selflessly, and well, and to endure and adjust to the lacks of the mate. We may be married to the mate of some other person in the group, but we can get practice with the one we happen to be wedded to in this incarnation. If we make a fairly good job of learning, we just might be led by our High Self to find the true mate and to enjoy a taste of heaven through the love and recognition.

I do not know just where or how the idea of "soul mates" evolved, but it is wide spread, and could well have been part of the secret lore of Huna which escaped from the initiate kahunas and became common property--with the usual misunderstanding and warping, of course. We read in literature of the ones who have left the ordinary love and found the ultimate and perfect love. The great poets sing of the perfect mate and the perfect love. But for the majority the dream is only a far and nostalgic hope--a dream seldom told or even recognized as such. We see men and women staring at each other perhaps "across a room," each asking, questing, "Are you the one? Are you? Are you?"

But if we find the true mate under the most ideal circumstances, the love is difficult to make perfect, FOR the low self of each of us is like the little brother who hides behind the sofa when his sister is courting. They rule the body and while the middle selves may be more than satisfactory in their likes and dislikes and their intellectual approach, the physical of each may be out of step and ready to clash. Fortunate indeed is the pair whose low selves also go together nicely. But still, we see instances in which the love surmounts physical defects and the love endures despite the physical handicaps. Always we practice loving, striving for the perfection of which we dream. If we can accomplish a near perfection, be it said, it makes little difference if the mate falls short. We are learning the great lesson that, in another incarnation, will admit us into the inner room. Keep your lamps filled with oil and be watchful, for who knows "when the Bridegroom cometh." (Women, do not let your love spoil your children, while you fight back your husband and keep him from disciplining them, and denying him love. On the other hand, husbands should take their full part in the rearing of the children and give the wife all the love and support she needs. The normal way of living is the best way. A lopsided marriage is a bad one.) (I have pontificated!)

We are dealing in these short talks with the general subject of THE TEN ELEMENTS OF HUNA, and often get far away from them.

You recall that these were the three selves, the three shadowy or aka bodies, the three manas, and the physical body while it lasts, but which is changed with each incarnation.

In the question and answer part of the last talk, I mentioned the expectation that we were about to have a Day of Judgment and that with the present population explosion the world around, it looked as though most of the created "souls" were now in the body, or were close enough in terms of an incarnation to be within easy reach of whoever or whatever may do the judging.

In the Four Gospels we have one version of the Drama in which Jesus, as the man--not then as the High Self--speaks of the popular belief that such a Judgment is right at hand. This is for the benefit of the uninitiated, and when the document was stolen from the initiates, it was, of course, vastly misunderstood.

In John, the 17th chapter, we find Jesus facing his crucifixion, but at that time he confidently requested God to bring on the Judgment. We read: "These words spake Jesus and lifted up his eyes to heaven, and said, *Father, the hour is come; glorify thy Son, that the Son may glorify thee; (2) As thou hast given him power over all flesh, that he should give eternal life to as many as thou has sent him....(4) I have glorified thee on the earth: I have finished the work which thou gavest me to do.*"

Elsewhere we read of his expectation that he will when "glorified" sit on the right hand of God and judge the unbelievers. In Matthew 26:64 he tells the high priest: *"Hereafter shall ye see the Son of man sitting on the right hand of power, and coming in the clouds of heaven."*

The idea in the Drama is to show the candidates for initiation that one of the great stumbling blocks to inner growth and progress is self-righteousness, and the desire to claim a reward for good deeds done. In this story, God did not respond when Jesus asked his reward, but deserted him, as he said on the cross, "Why hast thou forsaken me?" Could the Drama makers have written anything more telling in their effort to teach the lesson of selfless service and love and humility? Out of context, perhaps purposely done to confuse outsiders should they steal the script. And, Jesus as the man again, not as a High Self, got his reward--going up into a mountain, he was TRANSFIGURED and shone with a great LIGHT. Light is the code symbol of the High Self, and we see that he then graduated from the middle-self level to that of a High Self. This is the High Self who frequently is made to speak to the disciples and teach them. The Transfiguration should, logically, end the Drama, but it was needed earlier and so was used, but the death on the cross and the resurrection were what the outsiders went on, in trying to understand what they had no business to have without an instructor in the Mystery.

Later came Paul, to manufacture reasons for everything, with Jesus dying on the cross to save the world from the terrible sin of Adam and Eve, when they did the most natural thing in the world and discovered SEX. And he made this sex matter the Great Sin. What was a perfectly beautiful and legitimate Huna Drama to be played for the candidates when they came up for initiation, became distorted and mistaken for history. It was overwritten by those who copied the original scripts, and much was added that did not belong, while a little was lost. Whether or not we have all the coded parts is hard at this late date to decide, but we have enough of it to give us a quite different insight into the story of Jesus, as I have been at pains to show in my book, *The Huna Code in Religions*.

Have we a Huna lesson or two to learn from all this material? We have the greatest lesson that man has been given to learn. In the Drama we read that love of one's neighbor is a progressive step, but love of the High Self and of the mate is the superior love. This is a matter of constantly teaching and drilling the low self, which is an animal self and must learn middle-self ways so it can graduate into the middle-self life eventually. It must be taught to give up its greed and hate and savage instincts. It must be taught unselfishness. We, as middle selves are so closely tied to the low self that its animal desires are shared and hold us back. We must rise above them. We must at last learn HUMILITY, or else come back and take the lessons all over again.

* * * * * * * *

QUESTIONS AND ANSWERS

Q. What other Mystery Plays were there?

A. There is little information to go on in answering that question. The Greek Plays are the famous ones and little is known of what was taught. In one fragment a man who was initiated is quoted as saying that he had followed the training and had "seen the Light twice" while one of his friends had seen it once, and a third had seen it not at all. The symbol and code word for the High Self is "Light," and this is not just the Sun, which was worshiped in so many places as "The Light" and as supreme Deity; it is an actual, mystical experience which comes to those who are working to develop their contact with the High Self or to live the good life and to open themselves to Higher influences. We call such people "mystics," and refer to their experience as something MYSTICAL. Years ago, in Hawaii, I had been making an intensive study of sacred literature from around the world, and in the middle of a dark night I was awakened by having the mosquito netting which surrounded my bed flooded with a light so strong and so brilliant that it was unlike anything I had ever experienced. There was no sound to go with it, just the night silence, but I had a strange feeling that I was being subjected to some initiation or other. I just sat up in bed and stared and waited. In a matter of a few moments the light slowly faded and all was as before in the room....except that I was greatly impressed and set wondering. Since that time my correspondence has made me acquainted with a number of people who have seen this strange and brilliant light around themselves. It is very strong, but has no heat in it. It is perhaps a time when the High Self comes to be with us, perhaps to mark a step in our advancement. It is the one and only strong and really marked sensation which comes from all the occult studies and meditations, and once experienced, it is never forgotten. It is strangely impressive.

Q. How many times do we reincarnate?

A. There seems to be no definite answer to

this question. My guess is about twelve times for a fortunate person who learns well from each lifetime of experience. But there seem to be many backward people who learn slowly and remain bad and backward and hurtful. These may take a much longer time to learn their lessons of non-hurt--learn to be constructive and helpful and kind--learn to be "perfect, as the Father in heaven is perfect." The "Father," in this case is the High Self Parental Father-Mother. To be like it is the great ideal of Huna and success marks the point at which one becomes ready to find the true and intended mate, then, between lives, to be helped to blend the two separated selves to make one--a new High Self.

Q. Are we always either male or female in our incarnations, or do we change now and then and incarnate as a member of the opposite sex?

A. This is a question which has been answered both ways. Some of the most impressive cases of reincarnation have come from modern India. There both boys and girls have several times had memories of a past life that was so close in time that the children remembered other homes and families, and were able, when taken to the scenes of their former homes, to give dramatic proof of what they had said, identifying relatives and recalling things which had been changed since. In none of these cases has the sex changed. Despite the books written to describe a number of lives of some individual who remembers, I am of the opinion that unless one is born a homosexual and has his sex misplaced, the sex is always the same. Eventually comes the union and graduation to the High Self level.

SHORT TALK ON HUNA

NUMBER EIGHT

BY MAX FREEDOM LONG

GREETINGS!

This is Max Freedom Long speaking again and coming via tape to continue our discussions of the ancient Huna System of beliefs and practices. This system seems to have originated or at least first appeared in the glyph records, in ancient Egypt. About 5,000 years later the tag ends of it were picked up in the Hawaiian Islands, in the keeping of the kahunas--or Keepers of the Secret. From the fragments, and while making a study of the forces brought into play in fire-walking, it was discovered that they had preserved the fragments of a wonderful system of what may be called Psychology. But it was more--it was the science of man's being after death as well as in life, and, still further, it had a strong element of religion, in that it described beings both above and below men who were powerful and helpful. These ranged from Nature Spirits to the human beings who had graduated or evolved from the human level as we know it, and become Superconscious Selves or High Selves. (The Aumakua or Older and Utterly Trustworthy Parental Spirit Pair--Father and Mother, the male and female lesser selves joined and blended in them to make a more complete individuality of greater wisdom and power.)

Above the High Selves came layer after layer of ascending and still more powerful and wonderful Beings. These are beyond the reach of our understanding, and have only been postulated as a continuation of the upper growth or rising through evolution always closer to the Ultimate Power, whatever that may be.

In the great Drama of Initiation which has come down to us in a fair state of preservation in the Four Gospels, and which the Hebrews got from Egypt, we have some light thrown on the higher levels of being. Jesus, the leading character in the Drama, plays two parts interchangeably; first he is just the man talking, then he suddenly begins to teach as a High Self, often veiling his words in the language of the sacred CODE.

It must be remembered that the common man of the day believed that he could pray directly to God, the Ultimate and highest of all. But there was only one God and there were many people, all praying at the same time, so that God would have his hands full attending to the needs of so many people at once. It was a childish idea at best, but the true teachings were reserved for the initiates, and candidates for initiation were instructed by Jesus, speaking as the High Self, to "Ask in MY NAME." The Code tells us that the name is that of the High Self, and that we pray to it, and if we ask more than it can handle as an answer to our prayer, it will then send the prayer on up to the Great Company of High Selves or to the next higher level--to the god-aumakua or Higher High Selves.

This was enough for the candidates but when the Drama was stolen and was read by the outsiders, they failed to understand what was meant. Moreover, they thought they had found a history of a real, live man. They still clung to the belief that they were permitted to pray to God the All Mighty, but that they must ask in the name of Jesus. So, today, and as it has been in Christian circles for some twenty centuries, we end all prayers with, "We ask it in Jesus' name." Or we may be elaborate and say, "We ask this in the name of Jesus the Christ, who was crucified on the cross and who died to save us from suffering for the sins of Adam and Eve." Once we understand the coded teaching of Huna, we may find that we feel a little foolish when we think of praying in this ancient and time-honored way.

I realize that it is very difficult for many who have been brought up to believe in the old ways to accept the Huna philosophy. Habits of thought are very hard to break or alter. Huna is only for those who are ready for it--and they are very few and far apart. Fortunately, there are a few who are questing and who read other literature aside from that of their born belief. Or they have outgrown it and are looking with critical and questioning eyes at the multitude of teachings of the New Thought school. Frequently I have my reward when a letter comes to tell me of the delight of a searcher in at long last finding my books and Huna. It makes all the long research very worth while.

In the TEN ELEMENTS OF MAN, the matter of *PRAYER* covers the three spirit parts of man, his three shadowy bodies (call them astral or doubles, if you wish), and the three manas, which are really not bodies at all, but are the life force as generated by the subconscious self and used by it and the middle or conscious self, also by the Superconscious or High Self.

The central theme of Huna is PRAYER, and getting answers to prayers. I cannot stress too often the difference between Huna prayers and the ordinary kind--between the prayers made in the churches where the priest follows a set formula, or in the Protestant churches where the pastor closes his eyes, bows his head, and proceeds to tell God for twenty minutes how to fix the affairs of the world.

In the days when the kahunas were still at work in old Hawaii, they had a ritual in which the native priest retired from the sight of the people who were gathered before the crude temple platform with its several grass houses. He went into one reserved for "Braiding the Cord," and out of sight and silently, or perhaps with a chant, he did what in the code language is *u-la-na*. He took the aka threads from the silent worshipers who were praying for the good of the land, and braided or united them into a single strong strand which would reach to the High Selves who were watching. He made the mental picture of the land as it SHOULD be, and sent this as the "seed" of the prayer to the High Selves to be made to grow into reality. It was not a short or hit-and-miss prayer. It was a long ritual done under taboos of various kinds, and if the prayer was made right, the results were expected in due course of time.

Jesus said, "Pray without ceasing," and that was code. He did not use the word "braid," but *hoo-ki*, the root of *ki* meaning "to squirt water from the mouth" and telling the initiate that he must send the water of mana UPWARD to the High Self to help it to "grow" the prayer seeds.

The word for "braid" was *u-la-na*. The first root, *u*, is "I, myself," the man and is the root used in *u-hane* for the middle self. It tells us that WE are the ones to do the work of praying. The root *la* is "Light" and is the symbol of the High Self, telling us to whom the prayer is to be sent. the combined roots, *lana*, mean "to float," which symbolizes the flow of mana along the braided cord, CARRYING WITH IT LIKE A SMALL BOAT THE THOUGHT-FORMS OF THE PRAYER--the "Seeds."

This is dry and hard to get, but stay with me. It is the heart of magic and tells us that we have not made a mistake in decoding our Huna. They used SEVERAL words with always the same symbol meanings, always repeating the story. For example, *ho-ano* is the word in Hawaiian for "to worship," but it is code and the roots tell us <u>WHAT WORSHIP IS</u>. *Ho* is from *hoo*, the root for "to make," and *ano* is "a seed." So what does one do to worship? One stops trying to run the whole show by oneself and invites the High Self to join in the work of living--as is its just and perfect right and function. We do our part by making the "seed" and we then send it with accumulated mana to the High Self along the aka cord.

In the amazing double-talk or code we find most enlightening things which illuminate dark passages in the Gospels. I have told you that *ho-ano* means "to worship." It has, like so many Hawaiian words, other meanings, one of which is "to consecrate or set something apart for a special purpose," such a purpose as in the outer religion to be used as a sacrifice. What is it that we "set apart" when we "worship"? There are two parts to the answer. First, we make the seed of the prayer and, second, we "set it apart" or consecrate it by sending it as a prayer--the flow of mana that carries it being a gift or SACRIFICE made to the High Self to enable it to make the seed grow. (And know from this that the whole idea of pleasing God with sacrifices boils down to just this--to sending mana to empower the High Self to answer our prayers. It is the "wave offering" of the ancient Jews, I would imagine.

Here is a clincher for the other words: a reinforcer to keep us from missing the coded meanings of the Secret. It is the word for the ANSWER to the prayer and is *ano-hou*. Here once more is our root for "seed" and with it a root, *hou*, with several meanings, among which is "to make new or restore." It also means "to change a form or appearance," and "a likeness or resemblance to a thing"--this to change the situation to make it like the seed which was sent. And finally, it means "to pant or breathe heavily," in which we cannot mistake the pointing to the deeper breathing necessary to the accumulation of the mana which is to carry the seed along the aka cord to the High Self, to (as a sacrifice) make it strong to answer our prayers, to make the seed-idea grow into the hard fact.

There is a strange tradition which boils down to this: The united or blended male and female selves who graduate up from the middle-self level to become a new High Self are, still in a way like the lower selves in the body, in need of a form of sex union to start the creative act of making the answer for the prayer. We get this from the lore of India where they have many statues of the gods in close, sexual embrace. The true meaning of which seems to be that our prayers and gifts of mana cause them to come together in a slightly CLOSER union to engage in some form of activity which parallels our sex act in that it is the beginning of their creating something.

In the Four Gospels we have a coded passage in which Jesus says: *"Have ye not read that He who made them from the beginning, made them male and female, and said, For this cause shall a man leave his father and mother, and cleave unto his wife, and the two shall be made one FLESH? Wherefore, they are no more two, but one FLESH. What, therefore, God has joined together, let not man put asunder....All do not comprehend this saying, but they to whom it is given."*

We are warned as we read that all do not understand, that is, only the ones who know the code. Here our code word or key is "flesh." The word is given by Tregear as meaning "soul, spirit or power; (mana) force, energy, a god." This word is *io*, and it contains in its meanings a beautiful description of the abilities belonging to the High Self when "the twain are made one flesh" or brought into the closest union for creating the answer to the prayer.

Swedenborg, the famous Swedish mystic on whose work a church has been founded, writes in his *Arcana Coelestia* of his psychic "seeing" into the higher realms or the realms which we inhabit after death. He wrote:

"I heard an angel describing love truly conjugal and its heavenly delights, in this manner: that it is the Divine of the truth--united in two beings, yet in such a manner that they are not two but one."

He goes on to say that the delights and "blessednesses" of the heavenly union are beyond our power to comprehend--and fain would I believe.

Our American writer, Mary Austin, once studied the religious beliefs of the Paiute Indians, telling in her book, *Earth's Horizons*, of finding that they knew the High Self which she had discovered as a child and call "I-Mary" as the being who was higher and stronger and who watched over her. All her days, when she was in need of help, she called to "I-Mary" for it. The Indians also knew this higher Something and called it "Wakonda" or "Friend-of-the-Soul-of-Man."

She tells of asking a medicine man, "Do you TRULY GET what you pray for?" And he replied, "Surely, if you pray right." But this right way of praying involved an immense amount of explanation. To them, prayer was an act of OUTGOING on the part of the INNER SELF TOWARD SOMETHING, not a god, toward getting a responsive action in the world about you. They did bodily acts, danced and sang and performed an elaborate ritual. They felt that the Wakonda could not fail to fall into step with them and give the desired results--if the prayer ritual was performed with the right physical acts (the low self part in the prayer) and the right OUTGOING OF THE INNER SELF, which was the middle self reaching out to the High Self. They got rain and good crops, and general good for their people, overlaid as their prayer methods were by an accretion of cumbering dogma.

In the Drama of the Gospels, we have a number of coded sermons in the form of Parables. In one of them Jesus speaks in veiled terms of sowing seeds, and says, *"As ye sow, so shall ye reap."* He speaks of the seeds that fall on rocky ground and when the sun comes out, the tender growth is withered and the seeds die. This codes the necessity of planting well in properly prepared soil and then "watering" the seeds by sending mana daily to the High Self for its use until such time as the harvest is ready and the answer to our prayers is made to appear in reality and substance. The code word for "wither" is *lo-ha*, in which the root *ha* means to breathe hard, as in accumulating mana to send to the High Self.

I'll tell you a secret, if you take care to spread it far and wide. It is that if you can include another person in your prayer, or two others, picturing them as sharing the good thing you ask, you can also ask for the help of their High Selves and the answer to the prayer will come that much faster and better. We have always to avoid selfishness and greed and lack of love and sympathy with others. And here is another secret. If you have a feeling of guilt about something you have done to another person, this guilt sense may act as a blank wall set up between you and your High Self when you try to reach it with your prayer. But there is a remedy, and this is to go and make amends directly or in kind for that misdeed. Keep on making amends until your low self is convinced that it DESERVES to have its prayer answered. And a last secret for you. You can't hold a grudge and hate someone and get through to the High Self. Jesus taught us to pray in code. We read, "Give us today our daily bread, and forgive us our trespasses AS WE FORGIVE OTHERS." Clean your mental house and scrub and scour for dear life. Examine yourself for hate, jealousy, resentment, guilts and all the contaminating things. Get rid of them if it takes days of talking to yourself like a Dutch Uncle. Work to clear the path to the High Self so that you can begin to do the OUTGOING of the Paiutes. Sit down alone and think long about the High Self. Read some passages that you feel are inspiring and helpful from any book you favor. This will help the low self to fall into the mood. And don't be a "BREATHLESS ONE," as the Hawaiians called the white people who did not breathe strongly and accumulate mana and send it to the High Self. Take days if you have time. Prepare YOURSELF. Make ready your prayer-picture of what you and others need. Practice breathing your prayer and sending mana to the Aumakua.

* * * * * * * * *

QUESTIONS AND ANSWERS

Q. Just how does one breathe more deeply to accumulate mana, then send it to the High Self along the aka cord?

A. After quieting down and thinking of what you are about to do, and after you have decided on what you are going to ask for and have pictured yourself and one or two others as having obtained it and in the act of enjoying it, you can lay aside the picture mentally for the time being. It will be there ready to recall at a moment's notice.

Now begin to think of the High Selves and of accumulating mana to give to them as a gift--as a totally acceptable sacrifice--as the basic strength they will use to create the answer to your prayer.

With the knowledge well in mind of what you will DO with the mana, begin to accumulate it. Breathe deeper and more slowly and EXPECT the low self to do the work of accumulation. Take breaths in a series of four inhalations and exhalations, pause a moment, then repeat. This can be kept up as a form of slow rhythm until some forty breaths have been taken. The HA Rite of the Gospels means the Forty-Breath Rite. But the "forty" also means "many," so is not a set number. Go slowly and if you begin to get dizzy from too much oxygen, slow down. All you want to do is furnish the low self with enough oxygen so that it can burn blood sugar from the liver and make the added vital force.

As you get charged up, and you may notice this after even four breaths, you will find that your vision is clearer as you check it by looking at some picture on the wall. You will begin to feel more vital, more "up-and-at-'em."

The body has only one thing we can share as low and middle selves, and this is the automatic work of breathing. It is the one thing we can take away from the low self and do ourselves. We can't digest the food or beat the heart, but we can join the low self in doing the breathing job, and when we do, the low self is much impressed. It needs to be so impressed to call its attention to what we are doing and to be made to respond to do its part--which it knows how to do very well, as it increases the mana any time we get ready for a special exertion, such as walking or running. This is called a "physical stimulus," and is anything we may do to get the attention of the low self and convince it that something is being attempted.

Another physical stimulus which may be used is to take a physical position. The favorite one with the Huna Research Associates is that advised by Baron Eugene Ferson in his lessons. One stands up, spreads the feet wide apart, and extends the arms straight out from the sides, left palm facing down, right palm facing up, looking straight ahead with back straight. Ferson thought we stuck the hands and feet out beyond the oval shadowy body or double which surrounds us, and made contact with the "Universal Life Force," which was outside and filling the whole of the atmosphere. The trick was to draw in this force and charge the body. There is nothing to support his theory, but it makes a nice picture of something being done and gets the low self to work. Soon one will feel a tingle in the hands and while this may be lack of circulation, with Ferson it passed as the sign that the Force had been accumulated. And, by about then it should be.

Drop your arms, bring your feet together and begin to think about the High Self, then begin to send the mana, and in a moment more begin to recall your picture of your ANSWERED prayer and send it with the mana, thinking of the shadowy cord connecting you with the High Self overhead. You may succeed at first try, or you may not. Keep practicing until the method is easy for you.

Aloha,

MFL.

* * * * * * * *

SHORT TALK ON HUNA

NUMBER NINE

BY MAX FREEDOM LONG

GREETINGS!

This is Max Freedom Long speaking again, the subject being Huna and the TEN ELEMENTS which go to make up the man.

We have discussed the three spirits in man and the three invisible or shadowy bodies in which the spirits live; also the physical body while we are in the flesh. And, lastly, the three forms which the vital force or mana (as it is called in the Hawaiian) takes as it is generated by the low or subconscious self and put to work by one of the three selves.

I want to tell you the difference between the modern concept of the use of the hypnotic mana and the idea as developed in the ages past by the kahunas or initiates into Huna. Oddly enough, the mana as used by the modern man began as Mesmerism, and it is said by the kahunas to be very strong and very real, but is denied existence by the psychologist and the hypnotists, at least those not acquainted with Huna.

Anton Mesmer was a French experimenter who added to the gentle science of healing with magnets, current at that time, by carrying magnets on his person and absorbing the magnetism from them, as he thought;

then, when charged up, sending the magnetism to a person who needed healing. Once he had taken the step of using the acquired magnetism HIMSELF he began to get remarkable results. Huna tells us that he was expecting his low self to take on an extra charge of mana, and that it did so. But the wonderful discovery of Mesmer was that he could make the magnetic force FLOW from his hands into the patient or into a tub of water, or into a tree, there to remain static until a patient came into contact with it, THEN to flow into the patient and act to heal him. The kahunas symbolized the mana as WATER and knew that it would stand still and remain static in the shadowy body of a person, or in a tub of water or a tree, going into action only when SO DIRECTED BY THE MIND OF THE MESMERIST.

The projection is the key point of the discovery. If the patient is given a heavy accumulation of mana by projection, all at once, it may overcome his low self and knock it out of the body momentarily, leaving him unconscious. (This Mesmeric-Shock method was used by the kahunas to drive out evil spirits from obsessed patients.) Ordinarily, the mana is made to flow gently into the body of the patient and to carry with it the healing urge to set the low self to using the extra mana to heal a wound or anything that is wrong. The extra mana and the thought-form of the healer behind it calling for healing wrought some wonderful changes.

Mesmer, dressed in silk to retain the magnetism, came with practice to be very adept in accumulating low mana and in projecting it. He taught the method to others, and by 1784 had created a furor.

Of course, the medical doctors were against it, and many scientists. They, as usual, didn't want their preconceived ideas of anything changed. They formed a committee to look into the strange matter, and Benjamin Franklin, who was our ambassador to France at the time, was invited to sit in and pass judgment. Dr. Deslon, a student of Mesmer, went before the committee with a number of patients and made some spectacular demonstrations of clairvoyance and the healing of tics and other things. Most of the doctors and scientists refused to admit that any outside or inside force was being used. Franklin, however, was impressed and thereafter became much interested in magnetism in general. Even flying his kite into a rainstorm and getting indications of electricity from a dangling key.

I have before me a pamphlet printed in 1843 and in it he tells of the pamphlet released in American by Dr. Durand which was supposed to expose the new theory of Animal Magnetism as a complete hoax. Let me read what he had to say about the blast. "Durand promised an exposition of the humbug, and the bait was swallowed without mastication. The book appeared --an elaborate pamphlet--and went off faster than hot cakes at a hungry table. Everybody read it, and believed the humbug was exposed, though they could not, for the life of them, tell <u>how</u> it was exposed. The book is now irretrievably defunct, and it can serve no useful purpose, unless it be to singe a fowl, or stop some hole to keep the wind away." (I love his way of putting things. Can any of you very old listeners remember when we scalded a chicken, plucked off the feathers and singed off the remaining hairs by lighting a newspaper and swinging the chicken through the flame? Well, that was the way the chicken was made ready before cooking for the Sunday dinner when the preacher was invited.)

One of the main reasons why Mesmerism could not be laughed away was that through its use anesthesia could be produced in a fair subject and under this merciful influence painful surgical operations could be performed. Those who couldn't be Magnetized had to try to get so drunk they were dead to the world to try to avoid the pain. It was some time before an English doctor, a man named Braid, discovered that the same condition could be brought about, apparently, without the use of bodily magnetism, but by suggestion. This was called "hypnosis" and because it did not need to be explained in terms of magnetism, gradually but grudgingly was accepted by the doctors and scientists as respectable.

As some people could not learn to use Mesmerism or hypnosis, it was a great relief to the medical profession when ether and chloroform were discovered and could be used as an anesthetic for operations. Unfortunately, the use of hypnosis fell into disuse up to modern times, when a few doctors and dentists have revived its use. In our pamphlet we read: "Dr. Shattuck of Lowell has been a very successful magnetizer and lecturer, and has made some new and valuable discoveries in the science. A large tumor was extracted from the shoulder of a lady whom he magnetized, at a public lecture at Lowell, without causing the slightest pain. The incision was made to the depth of two inches. The experiment was performed under the direct personal inspection of three other physicians, who admitted the astonishing insensibility of the patient."

He says in starting chapter three: "It is universally contended by Magnetizers that all persons possess the magnetic power--females as well as males, and even children--differing only in degree. It is also believed that all persons can be acted upon by magnetic influence, differing, of course, in the degree of their susceptibility. In answer to the inquiry, 'Can every person be magnetized?' we answer--yes. But one individual cannot magnetize everybody....A lesser power cannot overcome a greater. The difference in magnetic power between any two individuals arises from the different amount of vital fluid in their systems; from the presence or absence of the intellectual and moral qualifications necessary to perform that operation; and from their knowledge or ignorance of the rules by which the art is governed....The power of magnetizing is greatly increased by practice. The operator gains confidence--learns to economise his power, and to exert it to advantage--and acquires a certain knowledge, feeling, or 'knack' which it is almost impossible to explain in language." He goes on interestingly to describe the method used with a new subject.

"The magnetizer takes a seat facing his subject, sitting knees touching, almost. He first placed the palms of his own hands upon the hands of the subject, and endeavors to establish an equal degree of warmth between them. He then places the balls of his thumbs against the balls of the thumbs of the subject, holding a gentle pressure. Then abstracting his mind from all other thoughts and objects, and fixing his eyes upon those of the subject, with earnest, determined, penetrating, but somewhat mild expression, he exerts an unremitted, unchanging effort of <u>will</u>, increasing in intensity the longer it continues, until the subject yield before his superior power, and close his eyes in magnetic sleep."

No suggestion in words is used, please note, for hypnosis had not been discovered or the word of it not yet spread. Here we see the accumulated mana of the low self sent with the projecting force or guidance of the middle-self "will" into the subject. He is expected to fall asleep, and the idea is telepathically transmitted, or he expects to go to sleep. Much of the effective hypnotic power is, in reality, exerted by the expectant subject in a form of self-suggestion.

Our writer says that the magnetized state is deepened by making passes with the hands up and down and along the body, and also on the top of the head one places the hands lightly for a time, also on the stomach. If time allowed, the subject was magnetized a few times for practice, then was ready for the painless operation.

Mana of two kinds can be projected from a healer to a patient, the mana of the low self, and that of the middle self. The "will" is the middle-self way of causing both manas to flow and move, and if the healer is highly charged, the results can be effective in causing healing.

Snakes were our first Mesmerists; having no legs or arms, they came to project their resident mana over a space and cause a bird to fall under their hungry spell. The magnetized bird fluttered helplessly, the snake came nearer and caught it with ease.

Some groups studying with Huna project mana through the hands of members of a healing circle and use their combined "wills" to make the mana flow into someone upon whom their hands are laid, and to heal them. In addition to this method, they may recite a prayer, such as, "Father-Mother, we hold this friend of ours to the Light for healing. Give him (or her) LIFE." One can compose a prayer that suits all, but once decided upon, it can be recited by the leader of the group while all members with hands on the patient remain quiet and hold a prayerful attitude of mind. Hold this for perhaps half a minute, then end your prayer in the way the kahunas did of old, "Our prayer takes flight. Let the rain of blessings fall. Ah-mana-mana." (Or use Amen if you wish. The idea is to close the prayer/action and not let it hand dangling.) Regular practice often will develop increasing healing ability, and frequently, if there are regular healing sessions being held, the disembodied spirits of people who were healers in life will be attracted to the sessions and help direct the mana poured into the ones to be healed so that healing is more direct and definite. It may be said in passing that unless the intention is to create a deeply magnetized state, no such thing will happen. Mana goes where it is directed and does what it is asked to do, if one has full confidence so that one's low self BELIEVES that what is being done WILL get results. A Doubting Thomas or two in a healing group is bad. If you can't be reasonably positive and expect results, better draw out and let the rest of the group do the work. Mana will travel or be projected, not only by direct physical contact, which is easiest, but along the line of sight of a person.

The help that one can give oneself with self-suggestion is also great, but, like other ways of projecting or manipulating the manas of the body, one must slowly train the low self and get it to understand what part it is to play in the work. A few people can use the art almost at once. The majority will need practice over a period of a week or more before results become apparent. Some never master the method for themselves, but may be helped by having another person sit with them and give the suggestions.

One may be helped to accumulate and use mana. Self-suggestion can help break down the barriers so that contact can be made with the High Self. This last is very important, and the kahunas had several words that tell us their preoccupation with the subject of getting the low self to contact the High. The aka cord along with contact is made is mentioned in code as "the path." The word in the code is "path" and that is *la*, which also means light, and is the symbol of the High Self. The word for "life" is *o-la*, or "<u>of</u> <u>the</u> <u>Light</u>." The path was also called "the way." Jesus, as the High Self, coded a great truth when he said, "I am the Way, and the LIFE." In another place he says, "I am the LIGHT of the world." But the blocked path also came in for attention. We read of the "stumbling blocks" in the path, and these are things which cause the low self to turn away like a naughty boy and told to go to the Father-Mother. He hides his face and dares not. He is filled with the sharp memories of all his guilts and misdeeds. But I have already told you how we make amends and give until it makes us feel that we are clean and deserve to be allowed to make the contact.

If one is making the most of life and needs no higher Help or Guidance, one is indeed fortunate. His prayer can be for more understanding, more wisdom, and more love for his fellows. "With all your getting, get wisdom," says the psalmist.

If one feels that his life could be improved upon in various ways, and if a determined effort is in order to improve it, then there is a simple way. It takes practice, but little more.

First, one must decide what is wanted in one's life, and decide to take steps to obtain it. Get out your diary, or if you haven't got one, get a small book that can be carried in pocket or purse--a small account book will do. In it write down the things you want to try to do or become with the help of the low self and the High Self. You will practice self-suggestion on the one, and prayer on the other. You are going to GET ALL THREE OF YOUR SELVES integrated or working together--which they should be but usually are not.

Write in your book all the things you would like yourself to do and be and become. Try to plan to make the most of your time, to study, grow in understanding, be healthier by observing health rules, be kinder, more sympathetic. Or to be more worthy of love. To correct bad habits. List them all, then go through the list and pick out the things you feel are the most important to you and those near and dear to you.

That done, try writing out the commands you will use in self-suggestion. For instance, "I am eating only the right amounts of the right food every day." When you get several commands worked out to your satisfaction, memorize them. Get the High Self to help by accumulating mana, and sending the thought-forms of the prayer-commands to it. Get off by yourself. Tense one or two muscles at a time and relax them completely. When relaxed, begin to recall your commands and to use them to command your low self to help. "Every day, in every way, I am getting better and better," was the Coué formula for health, if health is what you need most. In the relaxed condition your low self will accept the suggestions and act on them. BELIEVE that you are obeying the commands. That's it.

* * * * * * * *

QUESTIONS AND ANSWERS

Q. Did the kahunas use Mesmerism?

A. They did, very expertly. They could accumulate a large charge of mana and when they touched someone, knock them cold. Some American Indian medicine men did the same thing. The Aboriginals in Australia were mast masters at the art and candidates for initiation into the level of the "Clever Men," had to be good subjects as well as good operators. They used self-suggestion to put themselves into a light trance and then to go out in their shadowy bodies to distant places and learn things. They helped the police in modern time, knowing just where to look for a lost person or a criminal fleeing from justice. The kahunas used the large charges of mana as a method of driving obsessing spirits out of patients--for there are spirits, you know, and they DO obsess fully, or influence the living slightly or quite a lot. In my books I go into this exhaustively. It is important. Modern doctors use shock treatment for the same purpose, but won't admit that it is a disembodied spirit that is being made so uncomfortable by electric shocks or insulin convulsions that it will leave home. Jesus called them "Devils," and cast them out.

Q. How can we tell whether we are slightly influenced by an obsessing spirit or much influenced--or not influenced at all by one?

A. We have worked out a system through which the low self--who can see or sense the presence of such spirits--can tell us who is obsessed and to what degree. This system is called Psychometric Analysis, and I have a book about it under that title, if you are interested. The low self for some strange reason cannot tell the middle self directly what it finds when sent to examine another person, but, it can convey the information through movements of a pendulum. If your subconscious takes easily to the use of the pendulum, you can teach it to swing straight up and down over a signature if the person is being influence by a spirit. (Such spirits are called in Huna "eating companions," for they hang around and eat your mana to keep strong, then exert a hypnotic force to control you and make you do certain things--usually not very good things.) Once the "agreement" is reached as to the meaning of the straight-line pendulum swings, or of circles and deformed circles, the reading can be taken from a signature written in ink or a picture. The low self follows the shadowy thread which is attached to the signature or picture--even a picture printed in the newspaper--and in a few moments finds the one to be read, looks him over carefully, and is ready to report by pendulum and a clock face chart, over which the pendulum is held, just what it found. It will tell you whether the person is good and constructive or bad and destructive, whether he is obsessed to a slight or great degree, whether by one spirit or several, and about how intelligent that person is.

Some day we will have a good Psychometric Analysis reader on the staff of all prison boards to tell us what prisoners are really reformed and what ones will go right back to crime as soon as paroled. The low self has some very fine talents peculiar to itself and which the middle self can't match. Psychometry is one of them. Clairvoyance, with the help of the High Self is another. The middle self seems to be a very dumb self in many ways, but it can give orders and does so, taking all the credit for itself until we discover the skills of the low self. Self-suggestion is a way of cooperating with the low self and also with the High. If you can get your team of three selves integrated or working happily together, by means of self-suggestion or the Huna-type prayer plus self-suggestion, you can start rebuilding your life in a very large and lovely way.

And now, my aloha.

Max Freedom Long.

* * * * *